Daily Progress

A selection of daily readings designed to be helpful, relevant and reasonably short.

by Gary Stevens

Thanks

This is revised version of the book/ Once again it is time to thank those who have helped with the publication of this book. To my family: Jill, Hannah, Laura, Hassanin and Matthew for practical ideas and help, from the cover to the text.

To David Lowbridge for bringing the book from the computer screen to what you hold in your hands.

To the readers of the previous books who have encouraged me too, particularly Rev. Robert Wood. To Samuel Isuwa and others, who have given kind words along the way.

God bless you all, and may he use this book for his glory.

Gary Stevens

Spring 2024

Table of Contents

Walking

"I, therefore... beseech you to walk worthy of the calling with which you were called, with all lowliness and gentleness, with longsuffering, bearing with one another in love, endeavouring to keep the unity of the Spirit in the bond of peace.
Ephesians 4:1-3

Out of all the metaphors that the Bible uses about the Christian life, the one it employs the most is that of it being likened to a walk. As a lad I used to go to the beautiful village of Tostock, in Suffolk, to stay with my Aunties. I remember lacking enthusiasm for a walk; especially a winter walk. I would much rather sit in the kitchen and "help" my  Auntie make the dinner: it was warmer and much less hard work! Nonetheless I had to go, and dragging my heels, off I reluctantly went. However, to my surprise when I came back I found that I had enjoyed the walk; the scenery was beautiful, the nature on show was enchanting. And I was hungry for my dinner: it was a good thing to walk.

The Walk

Why is the Christian life likened to a walk? Well, for all of us life is a walk. Life, like the walk, goes through certain terrain, along ups and downs and tears and joys, until it comes to the end. A walk is a steady pace; you don't need to be super-fit, but you do need to be active. But, as in my walks in Tostock, it is great to have a guide and someone to point out things that you hadn't noticed and explain what they were. In life we need a guide, a sure destination and help to explain life's meaning. Bunyan demonstrates this in the Pilgrims Progress, and this booklet is called Daily Progress in tribute to that book. You and I each day should make some tangible daily progress to towards being the people God has called us to be as we walk, steadily, determinedly and purposefully, seeking to bring honour to the Lord of the Walk.

Walk and notice

What is a good posture as you walk? Stand erect, shoulders back, head up and put in a good stride. Move your arms for they will help you to move your legs (I've never understood why!). That way your body is the best position and you can see and notice what is all around you.

I mention this because it's easy to let the burden of life weigh our shoulders and for us to start looking down and drooping. We do not make much progress that way. Before long we've thrown off our kit bag and have flopped down by the wayside and stopped. Paul says we must walk: we must keep walking and we must walk in the right way. So today as you walk, look up at God's amazing creation. Look around at others and invite them on the walk too. Take care to help those struggling a little and encourage those whose walk is hard.

Walk worthy

What does it mean to walk worthy? Literally it means "appropriately". In answer, remember where you are going. Imagine you are going on a treasure hunt, with real treasure at the end. Think how you would walk then: there would be a real enthusiasm on the walk, checking the map, making sure you have all the equipment in order. Life's walk is a walk to heaven, to the place prepared for us. We ought to walk with that in mind today; today is a step towards the biggest prize of all. The path is mapped for you and the guide is given to take you there. What a privilege to be on this walk. So today, drop the complaining and the worrying and the sideways glance at what others have, and walk with gratitude, patience and a quiet confidence in the Lord who invited you (for that is what the word "calling" means) on the walk and will accompany you till the end. This way you will be able to put life's ups and downs in perspective and the things that the world has will be seen for what they are - cul-de-sacs!

Today, then is a stage of your life; a step towards Heaven. That is not being glum or maudlin but is the reality. As you go praise the Lord of the walk; seek to invite others along with you, and in all you do today, be careful to listen to the voice behind you that says, "this is the way, walk in it".

Prayer: Lord help me today to live my life that wherever we go together, I will honour you and bring you glory. Amen

4

A new heart

"I will give you a new heart and put a new spirit within you; I will take the heart of stone out of your flesh and give you a heart of flesh. I will put My Spirit within you and cause you to walk in My statutes, and you will keep My judgments and do them."
Ezekiel 36:26-27

On December 3, 1967, 53-year-old Lewis Washkansky received the **first** human heart transplant in Cape Town, South Africa. It seemed an impossible thing only a few years before let alone when Ezekiel penned these words. A new heart? Yet God had promised this operation nearly 600 years before Jesus  came to Bethlehem. Of course, the Lord wasn't talking about a physical operation but a spiritual one. But there are some parallels.

There has to be a need

Why does God decide to give the people of Israel a new heart? What was wrong with their old one? Ezekiel likens the old one to a heart of stone. Without stretching the metaphor too much this old heart was hard, cold and dead. A hard heart has no compassion; a cold heart has no love and a dead heart has no life. These word pictures illustrate what was wrong with the ancient people of Israel, what was wrong with you before you were saved and what is wrong with all mankind today. The fact is you can't persuade anyone to become a Christian: you cannot sell the gospel and you cannot educate someone to accept Christ. All need a new heart.

There has to be a donor

This is a gruesome fact, of course, but a necessary one. Denise Darvall, a 25-year-old woman who was fatally injured in a car accident, was that first donor. Her heart gave new life. When Jesus died the just, for the unjust, his death gave many, many people a new heart. He swapped his heart for theirs and so it is that becoming a Christian is never about a mental process but a metamorphosis: a complete change from one thing to another. The dead stony, cold heart has been taken away and a new warm, soft, fleshy heart is given in its place. That heart is Jesus' heart and the surgeon, dare we say, is the Holy Spirit.

There has to be a change

So, the cold stony heart is removed, and the new heart is given in its place. When this happens, the recipient can see what they couldn't see before: they understand something of who God is and what he has done. They understand also that they must come to Christ in repentance and faith, and he freely grants a full pardon for sin to all who do this. This is salvation, and salvation is a gift. Salvation then is not punishing you for your sins: or to put it another way; it is not giving you what you do deserve (that is mercy); and giving you what you don't deserve (that is grace). It is a legal transaction; it is a spiritual transaction; it is a felt and experienced transaction. We are never and can never be the same again.

Why then am I not perfect?

You are not perfect here, because the change that has happened is a foretaste of a permanent change that takes place when you leave this world. Prophecy has a future fulfilment and so does this. When you enter heaven, this change will be pure, perfect and permanent. Here we are surrounded by sin of all kinds and we are bombarded by an enemy with constant enticements to sin, and we fall, and we fail because this heart is given to awaken us to a real relationship with God, but it is never going to be able to be perfect until the final change comes. It's a bit like a deposit paid in advance. When the final payment is made we'll be home in heaven and all Jesus has done will be complete. Then you will enter in to the joy of your Lord and there will be nothing that will ever spoil or corrupt your eternal life of joy with Him who loved you and died for you.

Today, as you go out into the world, rejoice in your new heart. Be careful to guard what God has given you. Constantly thank the Lord Jesus for his "gift too wonderful for words". No matter what your circumstances are; they cannot change what he has done for you and what he has in store for you. Aim to share that good news with someone today.

Prayer: Lord, thank you for my new heart. Help me to be able to rejoice in whatever my circumstances are. Help me to guard my new heart carefully from anything that would make it unfit for you to live in it. Amen

8

Where is the Secret Place?

" He who dwells in the secret place of the Most High
Shall abide under the shadow of the Almighty."
Psalm 91:1

We are familiar with the idea of running to a bolt hole: perhaps the rabbit from the fox, or Jerry the cartoon mouse from Tom the cat. Perhaps you have been chased and you've found a place of safety: a den or a tree, a safe place where no one can get you; maybe your bedroom where you slam the door and put the chest of drawers in front it. Perhaps you have had one of those dreams where you are being chased and you are searching frantically in your dream for a safe place...

The danger

The psalmist knows all about running from danger: he mentions a fowler setting his traps; he talks of plagues; wars; nightmares, wild animals and many other evils. Today, I guess those dangers may not be on your mind but there are plenty of other things that may be. Do you face sickness, redundancy, family troubles, work stresses or sadness? Why are they dangers: because they threaten to overwhelm you; they threaten your peace. Perhaps they will make you doubt the Lord's love or goodness. Perhaps they make you worry that you are not even saved after all.

Run and hide

What the psalmist is saying is nothing short of amazing: He who dwells in the secret place of the Most High (El Elyon) shall abide under the shadow of the Almighty (El Shaddai). Where is

the secret place? He points to the tabernacle built by Moses as instructed by the Lord. Inside the tabernacle was the outer court, but there is no hiding place there; then the holy place, but there is only the candlestick and the table of showbread there. Keep running; keep running; where next? Next is the inner sanctuary; the Holy of Holies. Inside is the Ark of the covenant; above the Ark is the Mercy Seat and above the Mercy Seat are the two Cherubim. Everywhere is covered in gold and the glory of the Lord shines all around. Run to where the shadow is: on the mercy seat between the cherubim, and you will be safe. How so? Because that is where God himself has promised to dwell. Safe at last; cling to the place that God says he will not leave.

But you know perfectly well that only the high priest is allowed in here and that only once a year and that only with the blood of a pure and spotless animal sacrifice. How can I go in here?

How do I do that?

Let's face it you cannot physically go there now because it's gone. But the answer is the same as it was for the ancient Israelites: Psalm 91 is not obsolete: it teaches that you run into God's presence by faith; just as they had to. Now, of course, Jesus is the ark and the veil separating the Holy of Holies from the rest of the Temple is torn in two: it is open 24:7, and you can go into the presence of God for comfort and safety at any and all times. You can go there with frightened spirit and a fast-beating heart: cling to him and he will cover you with his wings. The secret place is that place where you put everything else away and come quietly and deliberately to God in prayer: listen to Jesus himself telling you:

> *But you, when you pray, go into your room, and when you have shut your door, pray to your Father who is in the secret place;*
> *(Matthew 6:6)*

The secret place is really an open secret: it is known but often not acknowledged. The secret place is the place where you and God are alone together in privacy. God invites all his people to that place; so why is it that the secret place remains a secret to many Christians? It is simply because we too often don't bother looking for it. Too many times we think we can walk the Christian life our own way. That is the way to an ineffective life. The psalmist teaches that the way to live your life is to *dwell* with and not simply occasionally visit the Lord. It takes self-discipline, but in fact that is the secret to living a rich and meaningful life with the Lord.

Today, run to the Lord; go to him now earnestly in secret; praise him for all he has done; thank him for todays' blessings; earnestly bring today's petitions. Honestly confess your sin. Ask that he stay with you today.

Prayer: Lord keep close to me throughout the day. Help me to run into your presence: help me know and feel your presence today. Amen

12

What sort of building are you?

" …you are God's building. According to the grace of God which was given to me, as a wise master builder I have laid the foundation, and another builds on it. But let each one take heed how he builds on it. For no other foundation can anyone lay than that which is laid, which is Jesus Christ. Now if anyone builds on this foundation with gold, silver, precious stones, wood, hay, straw, each one's work will become clear; for the Day will declare it, because it will be revealed by fire; and the fire will test each one's work, of what sort it is. If anyone's work which he has built on it endures, he will receive a reward...."

I Corinthians 3:9-14

The Christian is likened to different things in the bible, but this one is a bit unusual: you are God's building; made of living stones, built upon a living stone (I Peter 2:4-5). If you are going to build a building, then there are some questions that need to be answered. What sort of building are you? What are you made of? And before you start, what is your foundation?

The Foundation

Paul is writing to the Corinthian church. This is a church that excels in some things and is deficient in others. It is a church in a "hard area", as it is said today. Corinth was famed for its sin and the church had a fight on its hand to keep sin outside the doors. Paul reminds them a church is a building of God's people, whose foundation is the gospel, preached accurately, applied faithfully, accepted wholeheartedly.

But you and your life are also, God's building. Your life must have Jesus as its foundation. What does that look like? Jesus said:

"... whoever hears these sayings of Mine, and does them, I will liken him to a wise man who built his house on the rock: and the rain descended, the floods came, and the winds blew and beat on that house; and it did not fall, for it was founded on the rock."
(Matthew 7:24-25)

You start the Christian life by putting your trust in Jesus, asking him to forgive your sins and to be your Lord and Saviour. You repent of your old ways and, even though you don't know how it will work out, you embrace Jesus' way. That is your foundation; that is what you build on.

What are you made of?

As two of the three little pigs found out, your building must be made of the right material. But, what do you build with? Paul answers that question in this passage. A building can be built with all sorts of materials, but in the spiritual life it must be built of the materials that will withstand the fire of the Day's declaration. That is the day that we appear as stewards before Jesus to give an account for what we have done with the life he gave us; with the days he counted out for us, with gifts with which he equipped us.

But what is spiritual gold, silver and precious stone? Firstly, and obviously your life's building is to be of costly and valuable material. It is the brick of sacrificial giving, it is the building blocks of hours read poring over the scripture. It is the cement of prayer, love and sacrificial thinking and doing. These are the materials we build our lives with. These are the materials that will make a lasting and rewarding building.

The rubble of impurity, bad language, selfishness, pride, envy, gossip and whatever else we have slipped in unnoticed (so we thought) will not stand in that day. They will be burned, like wood, hay and stubble to our loss.

How well are you built?

It's good to have a big, strong person next to you. A little child will often put their hand in their Daddy's hand or their teacher's hand to help them feel safe. Are you a strong building? Are you good to have in the church? Can people rely on you? Are you a solid unit, well-built and sturdy? Or are you a spiritual jelly, or even flotsam on the waves. You're not sure of what you are, or what you believe, or how to live your Christian life, because you will not discipline yourself to build. You may point to a hard life, a brutal childhood or many other things as a reason why you are where you are. But we have a God who forgives, who heals and who wants us to build our lives on Him and his word. A solid bungalow is better than a weak castle, so build, little by little, step by step, brick by brick with God's manual as your guide and his Spirit as your instructor. And be amazed at what he can do with little builders like you and like me.

Prayer: Lord, help me to be conscious today that I either will build something worthwhile and wonderful for you, or by my neglect build something out of square or even nothing at all. Help me to build something you are proud of. Amen

16

Called to be a priest

" you are a holy priesthood, to offer up spiritual sacrifices acceptable to God through Jesus Christ... you are a royal priesthood... that you may proclaim the praises of Him who called you out of darkness into His marvellous light." **I Peter 2:5,9**

How do you fancy being called to be a priest? What comes into your mind when you think of the priesthood? Perhaps a medieval priest copying texts in silence, or an Old Testament cleric busy at the Temple. The apostle Peter probably had that in mind when he writes these somewhat surprising words, that you, the Christian, are called to the priesthood. What does that mean?

Special clothes

The priest had to wear special clothes; each piece had a special meaning. There isn't space to do justice to it all here, but the fact is you are given new clothes when you are saved: it is called a robe of righteousness: *For He has clothed me with the garments of salvation. He has covered me with the robe of righteousness* Isaiah 61:11 *(see also Rev. 6:11 and 7:9-14)*

A robe denotes that you are both covered, and well dressed. So, spiritually speaking you are covered by Christ's righteousness; you are wearing his robe. That robe is just for you and is the right fit. When God looks at you, he doesn't see your sin; the old rags of a sinful life; he sees Christ righteousness because you wear it like a robe. These are precious robes for they cost Jesus his very life to buy them for you.

You are a holy priest...

The robes also mean that you are set apart for the Lord. The Levites who were the priestly tribe, were told in the early chapters of Numbers that they were not to be numbered with the Children of Israel; they were separate; they had a specific and unique role. It was to serve the Lord in his temple night and day. They were set apart; sanctified. That is what holy means. You are holy, not because you are perfect, but because you are set apart by God for his service. That means you are set apart 24/7 every day and all the time. We are saved to serve and separated to serve the Lord Jesus.

...To offer up spiritual sacrifices

What was the job of the Old Testament priest? It was to offer up sacrifices. Thankfully for you, it is not lambs and bulls and so on, but, Peter says, spiritual sacrifices, acceptable to God, through Jesus Christ. What does that mean? In short it means that to serve God well, you must live in such a way as to please him and not yourself. In other words, live in such a way as to honour him who loved you and gave himself for you. It also means denying yourself, not doing what you would want to do, but doing those things that please God, help your brothers and sisters and advance the kingdom. What that means for you, you must work out today and every day.

You are a royal priest…

You're the child of the King of kings. What a status! Today spend some time reflecting on that incredible privilege. Once you were not part of God's people; now you are. Once you were bound for Hell, now you're looking forward to Heaven. What a wonderful change Jesus has wrought.

…Proclaim his praises

The Christian life is hard, but it is to be characterised by praise and worship. Do you sing out to God in joy and thankfulness for all he has done? You have been called out of darkness; the darkness of having no idea how to live, no way of seeing God, and eventually being thrust into outer darkness where there little else but wailing and regret. You have been brought to the Light, the Light of the world. You have a hope, you have a divine friend. You have Heaven all prepared for you. So, sing to God songs of worship.

Today, reflect on what it means to be called apart from the world and to be separated to God. That might seem strange in the midst of a busy, sometimes a frantically paced life. But you are called to be separate from the world. You are called to live for Jesus and for him before all else; family, job and self. Ask him to show what that looks like for you. Reflect on your priorities: are they what they should be, or has someone else taken Jesus place?

Prayer: Lord, once again I give you my life. Help me to put you first in everything. Even if I don't know where to start; help me to start. Amen

20

It's ok to cry

" ...put my tears in your bottle: Are they not all written in your book?"
Psalm 56:8

I wrote these words on the anniversary of the day my brother Paul died. He died as a result of the injuries he sustained in brutal car crash; one that was not his fault.

As the day started I looked at the clock and thought that at this moment on that day he was still alive, having no idea what was going to happen. As the minutes ticked down to the crash time, fairly early in the morning, I felt the lump in my throat getting bigger and bigger. Is it right for a Christian to cry?

We don't like to be seen to cry

I don't remember ever seeing my parents cry when I was young, neither did I see Aunts, Uncles or grandparents cry. And I grew up in an area where I didn't see my young friends cry either. So, I figured that crying is for weak people: it is not what I should do.

Another thing I noticed when I was young, was that if you watched a film where someone was crying (they had received bad news for example), they would begin to cry and then apologise for crying! Some caring fellow would issue the hanky, and it was understood that they were to try to stop crying as soon as possible. Even today isn't there a feeling that crying is a bad thing: something to be done in private if it has to be done at all?

Jesus cried

So, I was very surprised when I first read that Jesus cried. Even more so when you read that he cried in front of everyone; people he didn't know at all (as we say), friends, acquaintances, maybe even family. He shed tears; he cried. I always think that is quite amazing. How can it be that the Son of God would cry? He is the Rock of Ages. He is the creator. He has seen more deaths than we can count. Why does he cry? We read earlier in John 11 that he loved Lazarus with a strong love which great friends have.

But he was about to raise him, so why cry? Because although he was God come in the flesh, he was given the compassion and humanity of people like us. He felt the pain. He recoiled at the vileness of death. You see we were never made to die, but to live. Death goes against the grain. It goes against Creation's order. It is the sting of sin, and it hurts. Jesus felt all that pain that you and I feel and like us, he cried.

David the King cried too

David the great king of Israel cried too. And he asked why. I reckon he shed tears on many occasions. Tears because of his family situation. Tears at his own. Tears at unfair treatment and persecution. In this psalm he is being hunted by those who want to kill him. He must at times have got very tired with life. He had it very hard. He wants his tears to mean something. He knows God is watching, and that God loves him. Record my tears he asks. Write down how many I have shed, and why I shed them.

Remember those who have made me cry, and, in particular, make the enemy of my soul account for them too.

So, it's ok to cry. It's ok to weep bitterly at pain so raw you cannot express it. The key thing is that like David, we turn to God and not away from him in our anger and pain, blaming him for what has happened. We live in a sin-filled world, and terrible things affect all sorts of people. Maybe they are affecting you.

If you are crying, then take those tears to the Lord and ask him to write them down and remember them. Ask him to help you, guide you and keep you. He is able to carry you through this dark time. The pain will still be real; the questions will still take time to answer. But know for sure that God loves you as Jesus loved Lazarus, and although we don't know what he will do, he will do what he knows to be the best in your situation. That may sound glib but is the objective biblical truth. Cling on to it like a raft in the storm and go through your rollercoaster of emotion with him as your Comfort and anchor.

Prayer: Lord put my tears in your bottle. Help me to cling to you and not blame you. Keep me even if I feel alone. Bless me even if I don't pray. Speak to me even if I can't read your word. Help me to be sure in my heart that you will take me through this dark time. Amen

24

Spiritual Engineering

" ...all were numbered of the Levites... by their families, and by their
fathers' household... according to the commandment of the Lord
they were numbered by the hand of Moses, each according to his
service and according to his task; thus they were numbered by him
as the Lord commanded Moses?"

Numbers 4:46-49

I guess that Numbers 3 and 4 are not high on the chapters of the Bible that you read very often. Gordon J. Keddie[1] writes that it is a "painstakingly repetitive account" of how each of the clans of the Levites were to carry out their duties in the Tabernacle.

Set apart to serve

After the heady days of passing through the Red Sea, escaping from the evils of Egypt, a new reality had set in: the "new normal". Life had to be regulated. A new way of living had to be organised, and, as Numbers 1 and 2 show, the centre of attention, the focal point of the nation – the Old Testament church – was on the worship of God. All the 12 tribes were set in their place, four on each side of the Tabernacle, which was in the midst. The tribe of Joseph was counted as two tribes, Ephraim and Manasseh. So, one tribe was left. This tribe had no place in the army and would have no land of their own in the same way the other tribes would. This tribe was set apart to serve the Lord only. This was the lot of the tribe of Levi.

---

[1] According to Promise p.32

The price of service

Now I don't know how the Levites felt about all that. Were they upset that they alone could not own lands or choose vocations and feel settled down as all the others were? Their lot was in the minutiae of not just maintaining the Tabernacle but in the putting up, taking down, wrapping up and carrying it. It had to be done absolutely correctly or they could die. To them belonged the task of the seemingly endless number and types of sacrifices, all with their special rules. Why was this so?

Spiritual Engineering

The Levites were a microcosm of God's plan, and God's plan was very specific and very precise. The incredibly complex (to me anyway!) and detailed laws governing all manner of life and worship are there for all to see. That precision had to be there then: it has to be there now. Why is that so? Not only does the Lord have the lives of all 6-7 billion people in his hands; there are the stars, the planets, the weather, the animal kingdom and all those innumerable things that effect our lives each day. We do not believe in coincidences and that can only be true if God has everything, the whole world, in his hands. Everyday God orchestrates infinitely precise, spiritual engineering.

The calling of the Levites to be set apart entirely for God, for his worship and service was a sign that God loved his people and wanted the best for them. For that reason, it was an incredible privilege to be a Levite. Psalm 84:9 states that the writer would rather be a doorkeeper in the house of the Lord than to dwell in the tents of wickedness. This is a clear allusion to Numbers 3 & 4. That writer was one of the sons of Korah; a Levite whose forebears had been wicked. He knew what he was saying from his own family history.

For you the best can only happen if, as one of God's people, you follow his instructions carefully. The Lord writes the life manual and expects his people to read and obey it. Today, you are expected by the Lord to read his Word and obey it. He expects you to seek his will to make the right choices, from the right motives. Some of God's ways will chafe and not be what you want, because the still errant nature wants its own way. Today, submit yourself to God and he will honour you in ways you or I cannot guess. *"Those who honour me, I will honour"*, he says. Be a willing cog in the incredible machine of God's plan and see how he uses you for his glory.

Prayer: Lord help me today to seek a greater understanding of your purpose for me. Help me to trust you when I cannot see. Help me to seek and to submit today to your word and your will for my life. Amen

28

The joy of the Lord is your strength

"Do not sorrow, for the joy of the LORD is your strength... Be still, for the day is holy; do not be grieved."
Nehemiah 8:10-12

When you hear this phrase, what comes to your mind? It's such a contradiction isn't it? It comes in a surprising place too. It's neither from a psalm or comforting prophet. It comes from the strict and zealous Ezra.

Recognising wrong
The Jewish people had come back from 70 years captivity. This was a new generation, and a new start. But how could they make sure they did not repeat the mistakes of their fathers? They turned to the word of God and told Ezra to read it all, and Ezra did so, from morning till noon in the open square; hot and thirsty work. Ezra appointed teachers to give the understanding to the people of what he was reading to them.

It was noon; time for lunch, but as the people heard and understood what God had written, they were stunned by what they heard. They, the people of God, had not done as they should have. They began to weep and mourn. Perhaps they thought that the discipline of God would fall on them as it had their ancestors. They recognised, with tears, that they had done wrong.

Recognising responsibility
Whilst on one hand the people realised they had not kept the word of God, on the other the leaders knew that they didn't

know how to. But what would the Lord think of it all? There was no Moses or Isaiah anymore. The leaders had to make a judgement. Their judgement was based on their knowledge of the grace of God. That is interesting bearing in mind that both Ezra and Nehemiah had a track record of being very fierce when the occasion demanded it. But here they knew the heart of God was for his people. It was time to show mercy and grace to a people who were seeking the Lord. Those who seek him he will never cast out, is as true in the Old Testament as it is in the New. But it is a strange thing that they say: *Go your way... eat...drink...give... the joy of the Lord is your strength.* How can the joy of the Lord be their strength, and how can it be yours? Surely when you cry and weep and mourn, there cannot be joy? What must be true is that Ezra cannot be talking about emotion alone. Clearly, he wants to comfort his people, but it is more than that. Remember, he says in effect, where you have come from and what happened to change it, and where you are going now. It was true for them; it is true for you too.

Recognising joy is the fuel on which you drive
Every day you wake up go through a list of things. Call it a ritual, if you like, but don't let it become one! The first thing is to recognise that today is a gift to you from God. A personal precious gift. The next is to remember that you are a saved person. That too is a personal and precious gift. Then recall that wherever you go today the Holy Spirit is with you. That is the spiritual equivalent of everyday being your birthday. Who else has this? And those three facts don't change with how you feel,

or what you are going through. Allow those things to sink down into your consciousness; into your very core, and sing a song of thanks, pray a prayer of thanks, or say with David:

How precious also are Your thoughts to me, O God! How great is the sum of them! If I should count them, they would be more in number than the sand;
When I awake, I am still with You. Psalm 139:17-18

Christians of old called it counting your blessings. Rend Collective sing:

What's true in the light
Is still true in the dark

Joy does not depend on how we feel, but on who we are and whose we are. This life is a constant struggle and all Christians go through the fiery trial and the deep cold waters of trouble. That is why God gives so many promises, and the most precious perhaps is the one that tells us is that he always with us. Read at your leisure Palm 139 and Isaiah 43:1-3.

The joy of the Lord is your strength means that the fuel that drives your Christian engine is a deliberate fixing your mind on what God has done, is doing and will do for you. Fix your eyes upon Jesus, for the closer you stick to him, the deeper your joy will be. You won't laugh and smile all the time, but you will have a strength that will keep you going.

Prayer: Lord help me today to draw close to you and deliberately focus on the precious gifts of your life, your love and your presence. May it be that dwelling on those things will help me today and give me a sense of joy in my heart. Amen

32

The Lord bless you…

The LORD spoke to Moses, saying: Speak to Aaron and his sons, saying: This is the way you shall bless the children of Israel. Say to them: The LORD bless you and keep you; The LORD make His face shine upon you and be gracious to you; The LORD lift up His countenance upon you and give you peace.
So, they shall put My name on the children of Israel, and I will bless them.

Numbers 6:22-27

I love this passage of the Bible. I use it more than any other to close a service of worship. Its depth of meaning is stunning. It comes in the middle of writings about laws, and sacrifices, and details of Israel's civic and spiritual life. But in the midst of that the Lord tells his people he will bless them; his heart is set on doing so. The word "bless" *(Hebrew: barak)* is a word that is more than a word. To paraphrase one man: it carried a force greater than mere sounds, for it entered a man's life centre and changed it[2]. God's blessing will change and does change your life. This blessing meant a lot to Israel. The psalmist knew this, and echoes of this blessing are found in many places. Perhaps the best is Psalm 67.

A solemn instruction
The Lord spoke to Moses: the word is emphatic. It was an instruction. He is arranging. This arrangement is a solemn

---

[2] A. Noordtzij: Numbers p. 67

promise that the Lord makes to his people in the middle of the desert as they journey through various perils on their way to the land he has promised to give them. God voluntarily binds himself to his people. And we see here a picture of the Trinitarian God at work, a passage that Paul uses as a model 2 Cor 13:14.

The Lord bless you and keep you

The name the Lord uses here is "Jehovah". It means that the Lord is eternal, self-existing and unchanging. It is the name he uses when he is emphasising the covenant relation he has with his people. *I am Jehovah, I do not change; I am the Lord, I have called you by name, you are mine* (Isaiah 43). As their covenant God he promises to keep and bless his people. To bless Israel means to adore, to cherish and love them. He promises to keep them, to grow a hedge around them and protect them.

The Lord shine... and be gracious

To shine means more than to give light to you, it means to be light for you. Jesus is the Light of the world. But there is a richer meaning here. For anything to shine, there needs to be light. For there to be a light there had to be a flame. The Lord will keep you warm. But this is more than a gentle warmth: "I will enflame you" he exclaims. We might say today, "to fire you up", to enliven you: to motivate you as you go. Those two disciples on the Emmaus Road said their hearts were afire as Jesus walked with and spoke to them. God's presence is a strangely warming one.

To be gracious is literally to "bend to" you. The Lord is bending down to come close. He is paying attention, listening, taking note.

His motive is kindness; his favours are undeserved, generous and free.

The Lord lift up his countenance and give you peace

This tri-fold blessing keeps getting better: Literally, the Lord will advance to you his face. He will turn to you and not from you. Imagine a life without God now. It would silent, joyless and hollow. He is with you always. He will give you peace. To give peace literally it means he will be friendly to you. He will keep you well (*it is well with my soul*); he will look after your welfare. What an amazing set of promises, given freely and out of the deepest love.

Put my Name on the children of Israel

The Lord says to put his name against each child's name; to signify their belonging to him. You have my surname. Each and every Israelite belonged as an individual to the Lord.

This wonderful blessing is for every child of God; Jew and Gentile; all those who are in God's family, are adored unreservedly, protected fiercely, and looked after carefully. Today in that knowledge go out praising the Lord for his love, grace and presence all too wonderful for words.

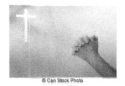
© Can Stock Photo

Prayer: Lord help me to know in my heart today, your amazing love, your generous presence and guiding care. Thank you that I belong to you, more than I even belong to my parents. Help me to revel in this wonderful love. Amen

36

Filled with the fulness of God

That you... may be able to comprehend... what is the immense breadth, length, height and depth of that which defies measurement; the love of Christ... that you may be filled with all the fulness of God.

Ephesians 3:18-19

It is easy to fill your life with many things: family, work, a hobby that consumes you. It may be a dream that you long to fulfil. As for Paul he cannot think of anything better to fill his life with than the fulness of God. But what does he mean, and how can you fill your life with the fulness of God?

God fills you with Himself

When you were converted the Holy Spirit had already begun his uniquely special work. He regenerated you; that is what it means to be born again. In the Garden of Eden, God breathed life into the form of the man he created from the dust of the earth and he became a living being, an eternal being. So, the Holy Spirit has done a work in you and you are "born again". "All things are become new"; you are alive to God and with God. But like an empty bucket, you need to be filled with the fulness of God. Jesus said:

If anyone loves Me, he will keep My word; and My Father will love him, and we will come to him and make our home with him. John 14:23.

God lives in you. This is what makes you alive. It is one of those things the Bible does not attempt to explain but expects you to accept. The Triune God, whom the Heavens cannot contain, comes to live in you. John writes:

And of His fullness we have all received, and grace for grace. John 1:16.

God fills you with his gifts

The Holy Spirit isn't a tourist. He is at work. His job is to glorify Jesus. His job is to instruct you in the truth. He is your guide. He puts his gifts in your life: love, joy, peace, longsuffering, kindness, goodness, faithfulness, gentleness and self-control. They are his fruit, in other words they are the outcome of his working in you and upon you as you feed on his word and drink in his presence in prayer and worship. To have the Holy Spirit live and work in you like this, is to have the fullness of God. The context of this prayer is that Paul has been speaking of the love of God. Paul prays that his readers will be filled with the first and greatest gift of love. Faith will be replaced by sight; hope with fulfilment, but love endures for ever, because God is love and God is eternal. How can you measure love? You cannot measure love any more than the Universe, or its Creator. But, although love may not be measurable, it is manifested. God's love is supremely shown in Jesus; in what he is and said and did. That immeasurable, infinite love is poured into your heart, as is peace and joy and all the other gifts. As you go on in the Christian life, making daily progress, you are being filled with the Holy Spirit and you are being filled with his gifts.

Are you filled?

So, are you? Paul prays that his readers would be able to comprehend the impossible; the breadth, length, height and depth of God's love. What for, Paul? So that they, and you, **will** be filled with the fulness of God. As you meditate on the love of God, as you grow to realise how incredible it is, you will want that love and all the other things that flow from that, for yourself. Jesus, in the sermon on the Mount, puts it like this:

Blessed are those who hunger and thirst for righteousness,
for they shall be filled. Matthew 5:6

You have got to want it, and as an American might say: "you have got to want it *real bad*". Hunger and thirst for it. Cry out to God for a greater and greater understanding – an experiential understanding in your heart and life of the love of God. That love comes to you from the Holy Spirit. So, to be filled with the fulness of God, means that the Holy Spirit, his character and his gifts take up a greater and greater share of the space in your heart and life. No-one has the right to usurp his place. He comes first in everything: in affection; in priority, in sacrificial living. Everything else and everyone else comes second, and you come last. It is the perfect reverse of what it used to be. Before you protest that you cannot put your spouse, or job, or family etc. second to God, let's face it; everyone else used to be second beforehand: they were second to you – now they are second to God.

Prayer: Lord, as Elisha prayed for a double portion of Elijah's spirit all those years ago, may I have a double portion of your Spirit. May my love for you grow today, and every day. Amen.

40

Accepted in the Beloved

Blessed be the God and Father of our Lord Jesus Christ, who has blessed us with every spiritual blessing in the heavenly places in Christ, just as He chose us in Him before the foundation of the world, that we should be holy and without blame before Him in love, having predestined us to adoption as sons by Jesus Christ to Himself, according to the good pleasure of His will, to the praise of the glory of His grace, by which He made us accepted in the Beloved.

Ephesians 1:3-6

One of the most heart-rending things in life is to be rejected, particularly by those who should be accepting you into their hearts. There are those who are rejected by their parents, laughed at by those they thought or think of as their friends, and are outcasts (in their own mind) in society. It makes them grow up without any sense of belonging anywhere, and it makes them ready, always, to believe the worst about themselves; nothing they are or do has any worth. It makes it easy and normal to believe any criticism about them is correct. Perhaps you are that person.

God chose you before he made the world.
Perhaps you have heard the old story of the two-part picture of a man walking towards Heaven. As he approaches Heaven there is a banner over the gates: *"Whosoever will may come"*. The second picture is that same man in heaven and looking back at the same gates. On the reverse side of the banner are the words: *"chosen before the foundation of the world"*. It is breath-taking to think

that you, were chosen by God to be his child before the world was even framed. That is, before anything happened to you, so you can do nothing to make God "pick you", neither can you do anything to make him disown you. Paul writes in Romans 8:30

Moreover, whom He predestined, these He also called; whom He called, these He also justified; and whom He justified, these He also glorified.

I heard a preacher say: "this verse summarises the history of redemption, from eternity to eternity". What does all this mean? It means that your salvation is not dependant on what you think of you, nor yet what anyone else thinks of you, but on God's eternal love *for you*. You belong to God, and that is that. You are **adopted**.

God chose you in spite of what you are or what you have done

Now, you don't need to have been emotionally (or any other sort of) abused to understand that you are not perfect. All have sinned and come short of the standards that God has set that he might be honoured in and by those he has made. Yet, inside we know the sin we have committed. We know what we have said and what we have done. And, also, we know what other people say about us. "You are a hypocrite" they say. You go to church for this reason or that, but not to worship God. Perhaps you have heard it said: "He / She calls themselves a Christian, but they do this or that". And it eats away at your heart. The enemy is never far behind, whispering the suggestion that on the last day the Lord will turn you away with what (to me) are the most frightening words in scripture: "Go away, for I never knew you". Do you picture yourself being dragged off to Hell kicking and screaming for mercy as you thought you had done enough to be saved, but it is too late? Paul writes: you were chosen in Him. In other words, Jesus is your passport into the country of Heaven. There is no barrier, no doorkeeper, no one to shut you out. Jesus blood has made you clean, and it is enough for the chief of sinners whether that really was Paul, or whether it was you. You are **accepted**.

Make yourself at home

As God's chosen child there is no need for fear, nor arrogance. What you have got you have been freely given, and it's given for ever. So, let the fear go, take off your raincoat, hat and boots and rest in the  armchair of God's immeasurable love. He loves you; he always has, and he always will. Rest here, be at home and feel at home. You are part of the family, you are a brick in the wall, a sheep in the fold. Nothing will snatch you out of your Father's hand: for your very name is engraved upon it. Take time today to think about God's unfailing, unchanging and unending love. Rejoice in it. Praise him for it. And then go and make him known by showing that love that God has lavished freely on you.

Prayer: Lord, thank you for your wonderful love for even me. Help me accept it as a free gift, even if I do not understand why you love me. Help me to rest in it. Help me to rejoice in it. Help me also, to spread it today. Amen.

44

Fight the good fight

Occupy till I come...

Luke 19:13 (AV)

Today it is easy to be a negative believer. The news seems to be bad; the church in England seems to be growing further away from biblical teaching and behaviour. And what about your church? When was the last time some-one came in, heard, believed, was saved, and went on with the Lord? Will the church become less and less effective until the Lord arrives to evacuate it from the earth, just before Satan crushes it once and for all? No. Gordon Keddie writes[3]; *The signs of the times are seen in every generation.* God is always at work, and he may come when the church in your country is flourishing or waning. We are never to believe that the arm of the Lord has lost its power to save and pluck us like brands out of the burning. Neither should we ever adopt a defeatist attitde to the Lord's work. Jesus said "occupy til I come", and of course he is speaking about himself.

The Church is a military thing
Keddie interprets this phrase as a military one: "take the high ground". In old battles it was customary to build your castle or fortress on a hill, as it was the hardest place for an enemy to take. If you were defending on a hill there could be no element of surprise: you

---

[3] According to Promise: Gordon J. Keddie p.203

could see the enemy coming. Then there was the sheer fatigue of running up a hill in full armour and weaponry. Marching to the battle was tiring enough, let alone running up a hill to engage the enemy. Of course, the reverse was true; you could run downhill with all that momentum full pelt into the enemy ranks and gain a great advantage. Take the high ground. It makes military sense, and it makes spiritual sense too.

Be a good soldier

Paul writes to Timothy: *You therefore must endure hardship as a good soldier of Jesus Christ. II Timothy 2:3.* Christians must not be passive, weak nor soft. Discipline and honouring a commitment have gone out of fashion in society, so it is easy to take that weakness on. A good soldier endures hardship, whether in marching, in training, in obeying orders and particularly in fighting. A good Christian must be a good soldier. A Christian soldier fights to take the high ground. That takes discipline. Discipline yourself to pray and read the bible and spend time with the Lord. Discipline yourself to cultivate good habits. Subjugate those desires which would cause you to lay your armour down. Be watchful in the company you keep, and the places you go and in what you read and watch. All these things give the enemy of your soul an opportunity to weaken you and render you useless in the Lord's service.

Take the high ground

Keddie puts it best: *"Spiritually, morally, in family and business life, in witnessing and doing good, in expecting blessing and extending love..."* prove that you are a good soldier. Life is all about fighting to take possession of the land. We are not to believe for a minute that the Lord has abandoned this world. As one lady put it to me: *there must be more people to be saved else the Lord would have come back.* The Church is not fighting a rearguard action is it? It is waging a war against an enemy who can lose his soldiers whilst at the same is unable to capture any for himself. So, not a losing battle but a winning one. But if you want to see the kingdom of God extended, to have more influence in the world, and to be relevant, then you must fight for it, for it will not happen unless you do. God wants soldiers, not nurse-maids in his army. So, labour on. Endure hardship like a good soldier, straining every sinew, and when you have done everything you can for the Lord and his cause, look for blessing, because in whatever way it comes you will find it, for God never asks us to serve for nothing.

Today, ask yourself: what should I be doing for the Lord? What should I be being for him too? Where and how can I serve him best. Today might seem an ordinary day but remember: God can do anything, for with him nothing is impossible. Attempt great things and expect great things today and every day and see just how great God is and how he will use even you.

Prayer: Lord, help me today to understand how I can be a good soldier. Help me to endure hardship as I live in your ways and speak for your glory. Help my life to honour the gospel rather than shame it. Amen.

48

Well done

Well done, good and faithful servant...
Then the King will say... 'Come, you blessed of My Father, inherit
the kingdom prepared for you from the foundation of the world
Matthew 25: 21, 23 & 34

A bit of praise goes a long way doesn't it. If someone has told you sincerely that you have done a good job, then it is immensely satisfying to hear. Conversely if that person tells you that you have done a bad job, it smarts. It is easier to concentrate on their words rather than your works that drew the comments. In this scene that Jesus paints it is very clear why these words were said and to whom. These words teach that you will hear Jesus say "well done". The question is will it be to other people or to you?

Everyone is gathered

Jesus teaches that one day the God of all the world will gather everyone before his throne. What that will look like is hard to imagine, but what is important to remember is the world as we know it will have ceased to be, and all the old laws of time, space and physics will have perished with it. All will be gathered. You will be gathered. It is a divine appointment that no-one can be late for, or forget "it's on", or refuse to show up to. Great and small, rich and poor, willing and unwilling will all stand before God. What a day that will be; painters of old have tried to pre-figure the scene, but even the best can do scant justice to it.

Everyone is judged

The burning question is: why are we so summoned? It is to a judgement throne we are brought. *It is appointed unto men once to die, and after this the judgement. Hebrews 9:27.* There is a day when Jesus is coming again, and he will summon all and his angels will gather all to his Father's throne. Those who have gone before will come with him. There the books will be opened – records of your life and everyone's else's life will be brought out into the open. Looking at the passage in Matthew 25, it is clear that God knows everything we have done, every day in every place and to everybody. That is an incredible thought, but it is essential to keep that in mind as you live from day to day.

Judgement is based on what you did

At first glance doesn't it look like the basis of the judgement will be about whether you have done enough good deeds? But we know that is not the basis of the judgement because a person's best deeds are counted as filthy rags in God's sight. By the works of the law shall no-one be justified. So, what is the judgement based upon? Well, in apparent contradiction of what I have just said, judgement is based upon what you did. That is clear from the passage. Jesus praises those who fed the hungry and visited the prisoner. But, as in every aspect of life, it is the motive that counts. You can feed a hungry man and make him feel ashamed and embarrassed. You can feed the same meal to the same hungry man and make him smile and dance for joy. It is all in the attitude and the motive by which you did it. So, it is here. Look carefully at what Jesus says; I was ... hungry... thirsty... naked... in prison... In as

much as you did it to the least of these my brothers, you did it to *me.*

Works done to try and save yourself, will stink in God's nostril. Works done to please and honour the one who loved you and gave himself for you are a well-pleasing aroma. This is the basis of the judgement. The folk who are sent away, had no concept, nor interest, in doing their deed to please and honour Jesus, but only to fill their bucket of self-righteousness up to the point where they felt they could use it as a ticket to heaven. It is all about the motive and the attitude. Jesus said: "you did for me".

Today make sure that you do your good deeds, whatever they may be with an honest desire that they please the Lord. Do not do them so people see them or praise you for them. Do it as a thank you present to Jesus and him alone.

Remember also that the verses immediately preceding this teaching in Matthew 25 talk about the responsibility of those to whom much is given. If you have been given talent, money, a good home, then Jesus expects you to use those things for his glory and the extension of his kingdom. Whatever he loans you in this life, he expects it returned with interest. That is more than fair isn't it?

Prayer: Lord, help me to understand the responsibility of using what you have given me, whether it be much or little in my eyes, for your glory. Help me to see how I can do that today and help me to actually do it. Amen.

52

Light

"You are the light of the world. A city that is set on a hill cannot be hidden. Nor do they light a lamp and put it under a basket, but on a lampstand, and it gives light to all who are in the house. Let your light so shine before men, that they may see your good works and glorify your Father in heaven.

Matthew 5:14-16

"Turn the light on", is something you say and do every day. But, imagine a world without light. Think for a minute as to what that would be like. I can't say "look like" because without light you would see nothing at all. you would go mad trying to grope around finding your way: you could never appreciate the beauty of a painting, a landscape or even each other. Parts of the Pacific Ocean are almost 7 miles deep; there is no light, for the sun cannot penetrate anywhere near that depth. But, amazingly some creatures make their own light. In that  dark ocean others see the light and are instantly attracted to it; and not always for their own safety!

Light shines

The whole point of light is to help us see. Once lit, a lamp or a torch or a fire can be seen a long way off. A friend of mine used to shine a light into the night sky to attract as many different types of moths as he could. The word "light" translates as "rays". Today, as you go about your business, your life will radiate light rays. They will shine through what you say; how hard you work; how honest you are and in many other ways. A light is not conscious that it shines; it just shines. Today you choose whether to shine by being true to your confession, or whether to hide your light under the bucket. To hide your light is to refuse to live the Christian life on Monday that you were taught of on Sunday. You hide it by being like the dark world around you; using their language, their standards. Imagine a world with no Christian influence: God has used his people to transform society in big ways and small; Gladys Aylward in China; Richard Dannatt, head of the British Army; John Laing, whose building company pioneered holidays and other benefits for the modern worker; Wilberforce, fighting to abolish slavery; C S Lewis the writer and Eric Liddel the athlete, among many to let their light shine.

Light helps

Jesus said: *"it gives light to all who are in the house"*. That means that by shining everyone can get on with their business. Light is taken for granted when it is on, and you may well find that people often take your goodness for granted. But doing what the Lord wants you to do will enable God's work to get done better and more effectively. A kind word here, a thoughtful action there can make so much difference to people's lives; even if often you never know the impact it makes. That impact should not be your concern, however; just shine.

Light cheers

Think again about how life would be if all was dark. For a start, people would be ill. People would be cold. Life in fact could not sustain itself. You need light; it is vital for your well-being. But think how miserable it would be just living in the dark. By being light for the Lord Jesus, you can cheer society, you can cheer others. There is a real joy to be felt by being around a Christian who loves the Lord, who loves others and who wants to be a positive force for good. Be of good cheer, says Jesus, the Light of the world, for I have overcome the world, as light overcomes darkness. By shining, you reflect his work, his goodness and his power.

Light must be lit
A light must be lit; a switch must be turned on; a fire must be started. All that involves a deliberate decision; a positive act. Today if you and I are going to be light in the world, you must decide to be so. It isn't easy because not everybody likes it; they have no time for Jesus because of the claims he makes on their lives. They will not submit to him and they sneer at those who do. Light shows up darkness; light exposes sin. Goodness will show up mean-spiritedness, dishonesty, lies and so on.

Today then, shine out; seek to please the Lord Jesus today in whatever you do; doing it remembering that you are doing all you do in his very presence. Who knows who you will help, encourage and cheer.

Prayer: Lord help me today to let my light shine; to spread as much godly joy and goodness as I can in your strength. Amen

56

Salt

"You are the salt of the earth; but if the salt loses its flavour, how shall it be seasoned? It is then good for nothing but to be thrown out and trampled underfoot by men."

Matthew 5:13

Come on, you've done it, haven't you? You forgot to put salt in it or on it. The dinner is served and it all looks good. The first mouthful goes in and you realise in a flash that there is something wrong with your beautifully crafted meal: it is bland. What do you do: grab the salt pot and shake salt on vigorously. That's ok if it is your meal and you are on your own, but what if you're in company and it is their meal? Or, again, suppose you are hosting and realise that there is no salt in the salt shaker? Oh no! You are condemned to a nice looking, well-cooked, lovingly prepared meal; but it's tasteless. Jesus said: *"You are the salt of the earth"*. What does that mean? What is salt? It is, as the dictionary might say, a substance with a characteristic taste, used for seasoning or preserving. If you as a Christian are the salt of the earth, what does that mean today? How can you be salt and salty today?

Salt is single-minded

It is only salt. Nothing else. You are a Christian and nothing else. Salt must remain pure. Mix it with another chemical and it loses what it is. If it gets mixed with dirt it is not fit for purpose. You must remain pure; you must not get mixed up with the standards of the world, nor in any way diluted, or else you cannot serve the Lord as he intends.

Salt has a distinctive taste.
Put salt on your tongue and you know exactly what it is: it's flavour is unique and strong. Salt does not all look the same: some may be white and fine; other might be pink and rough. Christians don't look, sound or act exactly the same, but all are taught by the Lord to be of a certain flavour. That means certain characteristics are to be in every Christian. A Christian should be loving; peaceable; gentle; kind; good, joyful and self-controlled. A Christian will not blaspheme God's name. A Christian must be honest and truthful. Living like this is good. It is pleasant; it enriches the lives of those around you. To use the metaphor; this sort of living tastes good. This will make the world a better place.

Salt seasons
However, salt in a tub doesn't do a lot of good. It must be mixed in with the food. You need to be part of society; you need to mix with people. You also need to be mixed in the right amount. Too little and you cannot be tasted; too much and you become repugnant: there can be too much of a good thing! Be wise as to where you go and with whom you go and for how long you go. Aim to bring people into your world where they can see what is good and wholesome and right. If you go too much into the world, then you are in danger of losing your saltiness and then you are no good to man or God and your testimony becomes ruined. There is a time and a place for salt: there is a right amount.

Salt preserves

I read that one method of salting meat used for many years involved pressing dry salt into pieces of meat, then layering the pieces in a container (like a keg) with dry salt completely surrounding each piece. If meat was preserved this way in cold weather, which slowed down the decomposition while the salt had time to take effect, it could last for years. The simple lesson is that the more you are pressing into society; influencing it for good and for God, the more the society you affect will be preserved.

Salt is sacrificial

Have you noticed that as you use salt, it disappears; it dissolves. As you work for the Lord in whatever way he has asked you today, there is a rule which is as true of you as of salt; you will be spent; you will dissolve. Or to put another way: He will increase while you decrease.

Prayer: Lord help me today to be salt and be salty. I may not be to everyone's taste; but help me to go and do what I was created and redeemed for. Amen.

60

Run...the race

"Let us lay aside every weight, and the sin which so easily ensnares us, and let us run with endurance the race that is set before us, looking unto Jesus, the author and finisher of our faith, who for the joy that was set before Him endured the cross, despising the shame.

Hebrews 12:1-3

Your life as a Christian is likened to many things; a walk, a journey, being a soldier and so on. But here it is likened to a race. The race is a long endurance test and each day is a stage in the race. Sometimes it is up mountains, sometimes on the flat and sometimes running gleefully downhill. In the days when the first Hebrews read this letter the race which everybody knew about was the race in the Olympic stadium. The athlete entered the stadium and raced. When you became a Christian, you entered a race. Who are you racing against: against the spiritual elements; against the enemy of our soul. It is not so much a speed contest but an endurance one. Your aim is to run all the way to Heaven. Those of a certain age might remember that TV show *"Gladiators"* where the gladiators aim was to stop the contenders from getting to their goal. The enemy's aim is to knock  you over, so you get discouraged, or knock you down so you don't run at all, or knock you sideways so you get lost.

Race...your race

The race you run is your race and your race alone. But you do not race against other Christians, trying to be better than them. No, you run the race marked out for you. It's your particular and unique obstacle course. In other words: God is sending you along a particular path at a particular time for a particular reason.

Race... stripped

The athletes of the time stripped down to the bare essentials; a loin cloth. Apart from anything else it served to say that athlete was completely single-minded and focussed on the race; nothing else can distract from what that athlete is doing. The text says that you need to be similarly single-minded: you are to "lay aside every weight, and the sin that so easily ensnares". What are the Christian's race essentials? Start off by confessing your sins to Jesus; they are like a net around your feet. You cannot run well with sin. Confess and deal with it before you start the day or end it. Then carefully examine your life; your priorities, your loves, your past, your distractions. These are your weights. To what extent do they help you run your race or hinder it? Today is the day to deal with them; ask the Lord to show you clearly how to prioritise, what to keep and what to lay down. Remember that you are, after all, running home to Jesus Himself. How many of those things you are running with will count for anything then? So, run with patience; steadily, carefully and deliberately.

Race... inspired

Be inspired by Jesus and the race he ran. His race was the first race, for he is the author of your faith. He loved you so much that he humbled himself; he suffered at the hands of those he had lovingly made, and he went to the cross. He despised its shame, meaning he willingly embraced it, so he could finish the race God gave Him to run. If Jesus ran a race only he could run, for you, then surely, you should aim today to run your race for him.

Now, maybe you have no difficulty with believing that Jesus was given a race to run – a unique race; but really is your race that important that nobody else can run that race? Can you make a unique and valuable contribution to the kingdom of heaven; to God himself and the church? Paul writes that you can. Beth Redman writes: *"I feel so privileged and validated that no one else can do the job He has for me!"*[4]

Today, be inspired to run your race for his glory, and race today patiently, enduring the stuff that the enemy throws at you, the blows he rains down upon you, the roars of derision he assaults you with. You are running to Jesus, to his arms and his smile and his "Well done". Be inspired to run to him today.

Prayer: Lord help me to run my race, looking at you and not at what others have or are. Help me to be inspired and motivated by the fact you have a particular role for me. Amen.

---

[4] God knows my name; p. 79

Tongue – our contradiction

No man can tame the tongue. It is an unruly evil, full of deadly poison. With it you bless our God and Father, and with it you curse men, who have been made in the similitude of God. Out of the same mouth proceed blessing and cursing. My brethren, these things ought not to be so.

James 3:8-10

The two-minded tongue

I am a Gemini - apparently! When I was young, I was told by a rather tactless relative, into astrology, that being a Gemini meant that I would have a split personality. You can imagine the angst that caused as I grew up! But there is a sense that Christians have two sides. As a Christian, you are seeking to honour God in all you do, and of course your old nature is striving against all that. This battle is supremely played out through your tongue. James is his usually robust self when he bluntly reminds us that the tongue is an unruly evil, full of deadly poison! Why is that so?

It is capable of terrible evil

With the tongue you can wound and maim and destroy. Wars start, feuding starts, families divide, churches split. Think for instance how there came to be so many non-Conformist denominations. Shakespeare captured the power of the tongue to do unspeakable evil in his play *King Lear,* where two of his daughters flatter the king for his kingdom, whilst the truthful daughter is cast out.

It is unpredictable

The problem with the tongue is that you never know where you are with it. Out of the same mouth comes cursing and blessing; you bless and praise God, and then curse and criticise those whom He has made and even those whom he has saved. How can that be? It is so because you do have two natures; in fact, you have two armies at war in your mind and soul. The Holy Spirit leads the one army which is all about seeking to put to death the other. The enemy of your soul, on the other side, knowing your weaknesses, will try and entice you back to sin by reminding you how good it is, to say and do this or that. And of course, add into the mix the pride inside which just will NOT admit you are wrong!

It needs respecting

If you are going to get a grip of your tongue (not physically although it might be a good idea sometimes!), then you need to respect what it can do – what you can do - because our tongues are really reflections of our inmost being aren't they?

See how James illustrates it: the tongue is like a ship's rudder; a small thing that can turn a ship which can be over a quarter of a mile long. Or again it is a spark which sets the forest on fire. That word fire literally translates as lightning strike. That is how quickly

the fire can be started. you have seen those pictures of forest fires, haven't we? Just one tiny spark. And in our verses above, it is likened to a cup of poison; toxic, seemingly harmless but deadly. Today, remember what damage your tongue can do, and that
will help you to be very careful what you say and how you say it.

It needs training

Like any muscle whether it be physical or spiritual, the tongue needs training. How you do that is down to you. It has been well said: that you have two eyes, two ears and one mouth: and that you should use them in that proportion. James says, be slow to speak and quick to listen. That one strategy will make a difference. Today, then, reflect on how powerful the tongue can be, what good you can do with it, and what trouble you can cause. Remember, metaphorically speaking, that you hold a dynamic tool in your hands and that you must use it with the greatest of care. Ask the Lord for help to use your tongue well today; for his honour and pleasure; for his praise and his glory. Remember that every word you speak is heard in the throne room of heaven, to the Lord on that throne you must give an account for each idle word.

Prayer: Lord help me to use my tongue wisely today. Help me to ask you for the right words before I speak. Amen

68

A glimpse of glory

In the year that King Uzziah died, I saw the Lord sitting on a throne,
high and lifted up, and the train of His robe filled the temple.
Above it stood seraphim; each one had six wings: with two he
covered his face, with two he covered his feet, and with two he
flew. And one cried to another and said: "Holy, holy, holy is the
LORD of hosts; The whole earth is full of His glory!"
Isaiah 6:1-3

In chapter 6 Isaiah has his life changed forever: He is shown a
glimpse of God's glory. He sees the Lord: majestic; exalted and
worshipped by wonderful angelic beings. Isaiah is shown God's
holiness. This was so impressed on his heart and mind that this
vision framed Isaiah's language in the rest of his book: he refers
to God as the "Holy One" on 30 occasions. Your experience of
God forms your vocabulary of him. The moment Isaiah is
confronted with God's holiness he declares himself a sinner. He
felt his uncleanness, and his
unworthiness to be in the same place
as this awesome holy God. But then
you read something quite amazing:
there was no blood sacrifice made, but
as an answer to Isaiah's own dilemma:
the seraph takes a hot coal and purges
his unclean lips of their purity; fire being the refining mechanism
for getting rid of the dross. Isaiah's sin is atoned for, he is made
right with and made fit for a conversation with Almighty God.

Isaiah's task

After this Isaiah duly volunteers for the task God had for him and he is commissioned by the Lord to go and preach to the obstinate unruly house of Israel. In honesty the Lord tells him plainly what the job entails. Go and make this people dull, deaf, blind and hard until their measure of judgement is full up. Isaiah, your ministry is a judgement, for my people have been told many times, in many ways but they have continued to reject my word.

Isaiah is obviously stunned at this. Like all true Israelites he longed to see God restoring his people to the glory years of David. He asks: "How long am I to preach like this Lord?" The answer is until judgement comes. Israel will be decimated. There will be a remnant remaining, and even that will be decimated too. All that will be left of the tree of Israel will be a stump. It is a grim promise, but at least there is hope of something. A stump doesn't sound like much, but you know a stump can grow into a beautiful tree again. Whilst there was that amount of life in Israel there was hope. Later, Isaiah was to prophesy of this stump as even smaller; a root (Isa 11:1), and he was to use this metaphor as a sign of hope for Israel. All these years later and you know that God honoured that promise. Firstly, Israel has been preserved in a tremendous and miraculous way. There is no Babylonian nor Assyrian empire. Greece, Persia and Rome's empires have come and gone, but Israel remains. God is faithful, and God keeps his word.

Your task

What about you today? Spend a moment thinking about God in his Temple, high and lifted up; majestic and holy. What must that have been like? Contrast that with your smallness and your sinfulness and ask the Lord again for mercy. Praise God that your atonement isn't a live hot coal on your lips, but something more wonderful: the substitutionary death of Jesus Christ; the Son of God. This baby of Bethlehem grew to be the man who would die, the just for the unjust to bring you to God. He is alive, and he reigns with supreme authority. One day, on a day of God's appointing, Jesus will return.

Today you have a message to go out with. It is more complete than Isaiah's, and you may be received in the same way as he was. Don't let that put you off. The stark truth for those you will meet today is that there is coming a day when Jesus will return and judge them. But, you carry a real message of hope, not merely judgement: There was nothing that Isaiah could really offer his people, for judgement was fixed and final. But you have a message which is simply this: that if men, women and young people will turn to the Lord in repentance and trust, then they will be accepted by God himself. They will not only be accepted, but they will be pardoned, and welcomed and loved forever by the greatest of Fathers, by the kindest of Brothers in Jesus Christ.

Prayer: Lord help me have a real sense of your glory, holiness and greatness today. Help that to shape what I do and say, to your glory today. Amen

72

Job's silence

Now when Job's three friends heard of all this adversity that had come upon him, each one came from his own place: Eliphaz... Bildad... and Zophar. They sat down with him on the ground seven days and seven nights; no one spoke a word to him, for they saw that his grief was very great.

Job 2:11-13

The story of Job's sufferings is the benchmark for which suffering is measured. No matter what you have suffered, when you look at Job you see someone who has trod that path bitterly before you did, and you shrink from his agony and hope secretly and fervently you're not next in the firing line. Job lost his livestock and wealth; he lost his servants and he lost all his children. In losing those he lost his dignity and his reputation, for it was assumed that a good man would not have been allowed to suffer like this. As if this wasn't enough, he lost his health and he had to go and sit on the ash-heap to scrape the skin from his itching, biting, disgusting sores. Seriously, what else could happen? One thing: his own dear and obviously grief-stricken wife, told him to curse God and die.

We are given a glimpse of the scene in heaven that precedes all this. But to add to Job's mental torture he simply could not see any sense in what was happening. He knew he wasn't perfect, but he also knew these things had not happened because he was living a rebellious life against the Lord. He loved the Lord and he worshipped him even after the news of his children's death. So why this was happening, he could not know and that gave him a mental agony he could not assuage.

What Satan wanted

What was Satan after in all this? You can see chillingly how much he hates God's people. What he wanted was to hear Job turn on God and curse him (Job 1:11; 2:5; 2:9). Satan's greatest delight is to see people curse God, blame God, and turn in rage against God. He knows the greatest prize he can have is to wreck God's honour; no better way to do that than to get his own children to turn against him. Perhaps the measure of any society is how it uses or misuses God's Name.

But Job doesn't fall for it: (Job 1:20) he worships. Job 2:10; *"In all this Job did not sin with his lips"*. Satan was thwarted, but what about Job?

Job is silent

When you read of the sufferings of Job have you ever taken notice of what happens at the end of chapter 2? The sufferings are well known; the conversations are not so well known, although the golden verses in them are. The ending too is well known. But before any of that starts Job left his house and sat down on the ash-heap and scrapes his sores. He sits down for seven days and seven nights and he doesn't say a word. He doesn't sleep; or eat or even drink, as far as you can read in the text. He doesn't pray. He doesn't acknowledge the comfort of his friends. He grieves in bleak, agonised, astonished silence.

Sitting on the ash heap

It's true isn't it that although you will walk *through* the valley (Psalm 23), it's still a valley? Pain is always painful. Although you are a child of God you may well be hurt, bereaved, abused, lied to, lied about, ignored and ill. In those times there is no answer, no relief and no explanation; just raw grief, bitter tears and black silence. *God didn't speak a word to Job.* That's the real Christian life. Job's story tells us that in this world we shall have tribulation, and it isn't realistic to carry on regardless as if pain shouldn't really affect us. Reading some writers, it seems that all you need is to pray a prayer, read a good book or hear a stirring sermon and you are up and away. That wasn't Job's experience, and whilst God <u>can</u> do anything, I doubt it will be yours. There is a time to grieve. There is a time to stop and sit down. Job sat down for seven days; you might need to sit for many more.

Today the comfort you have is that God cares for you, loves you, puts your tears in his bottle and writes down the date: Satan will answer for every single one. In that knowledge, cry unashamedly, but keep hoping, trusting; and walking through the valley, for one day you *will* come to the other side. What that will look like I don't know, but Job did come once again to smile, to laugh and be joyful again. In God's time I trust you will too.

Prayer: Lord help me today to put my hand in your hand and walk with you. Help me to know that you really are with me now. Amen

God knows *your* name

"Fear not, for I have redeemed you; I have called you by your name; You are Mine. When you pass through the waters, I will be with you; And through the rivers, they shall not overflow you. When you walk through the fire, you shall not be burned, Nor shall the flame scorch you. For I am the LORD your God, The Holy One of Israel, your Saviour.

Isaiah 43:1-3

Can you imagine life without your name? Perhaps you have been addressed so often as "Oi, you...." that you wonder if you have one! Perhaps you really don't like your name, and have asked, "why did I have to have this name?" Yet our names are very important. I was reminded of this by the title of Beth Redman's inspirational book "God knows my name". She points to Isaiah 43, and talks about how important it is to know that you have a name.

In the text above the Lord speaks through Isaiah to Hezekiah, the king of little Judah. They are surrounded by much bigger fish: the Assyrian empire, Egypt, and soon Babylon will be on the rise; the next great power. As it turned out there was only one godly king after Hezekiah: the ill-fated Josiah and that was the end of the Monarchic period of Judah forever. How could they ever dream of being of value to the Lord again?

Named and known

Yet, during that gloom, the Lord tells his people, for that is what they are, not to fear. No matter how bleak it looks there is no reason to be afraid. Now of all the reasons to not be afraid there may be out there, I doubt that the words Isaiah spoke would have come up on the list of inspirational things to say. But, what God says is really important. Remember, he says, that I created you, I formed you. I know you and I know you intimately and totally. I am your Father. I have given you your name.

Named and loved

To have a name means you have an identity. You suddenly change from an unknown and faceless thing into a person who is unique. When a baby is born prematurely, or when there are problems and the mother cannot hold her baby, it is placed out of reach and named with a label "Baby Smith". It doesn't really have a name, or an identity. But once all is well and the baby is home and named, it takes its place in the family, in society. To have a name means you have worth and value; God says to his people: "you are mine"; 43:1. "You were precious in my sight; I have [already and always] loved you." 43:4. You belong.

Named and valued

What is the Lord saying here? He is explaining to the people of Judah that because he made them, knows them, loves them, that they matter to him. Their names are written, engraved in fact (think for a moment what that would literally entail), on the palms of his hands. It means they are in a relationship with him that can never be broken. In any relationship with another you will walk and talk and listen and share with that person. For it to **be** a relationship it has to be two ways. That is exactly what the Lord does with his people. They are secure in his love. You as a Christian are one of God's people today and Isaiah's words are as true of you as they were of them.

Named and secure

Nothing can pluck you out of God's hand; he holds on to you too tightly; he never forgets you are there. Yes, you will go through tough times, through the waters (v 2) through the flames (v 2) through dispersion (v 6) but he'll never you let go. Beth Redman points us to Psalm 139 as proof; read it and see how intimately God knows you, loves you, and is involved in everything you are and do.

Today, whatever you face, go in confidence with a quiet and settled joy knowing the greatest person in the universe is your unfailing Father and friend. He holds your hand, he smiles with joy as he looks at you. He has got your back. He will walk with you today if you will walk with Him.

Prayer: Lord help me to rejoice today in your unfailing and unconditional love for me. Let that joy spill over for your glory. Amen

Spiritual Sweat

The fruit of the Spirit is love, joy, peace, longsuffering, kindness, goodness, faithfulness, gentleness, self-control, against such things there is no law.

Galatians 5:22

One year I decided that I would grow fruit and veg in the garden. I dug the soil, manured it, and planted all the seeds. To my disgust I got a spoonful of peas; the gooseberries got the blight; the raspberries came up blind, the blackcurrants produced as much as the peas, and one day the chickens got out and ate my cabbages. Not a leaf remained.

Although there may have been a hint of misfortune in it all, when I had a bit of a think it wasn't hard to see why it all went wrong: I hadn't watered them regularly, weeded around them, nor put nets on when the fruit was growing. In the end the fruit I got probably reflected the effort I put in.

The principle of growing fruit

To grow fruit, you must work hard. Sweat is the legacy of Adam. There must be digging, planting, watering, weeding, protecting etc. The environment needs to be right. These are the principles of growing fruit. But it is also true in the spiritual realm. You must sweat! You must think, plan, and give attention to detail. You must guard against pests, vermin and weeds. If you are going to be fruitful you need to want it, to work for it and to persevere at it. And you need your Heavenly Gardener's help.

The point of growing fruit

What is the point of growing fruit? You may ask that more often as you are trying to do it! People grow fruit to eat it, or for others to enjoy it. You may grow it to exhibit it, or to give it to others who don't have enough. Ultimately, you grow fruit to be productive; to enjoy achieving something. There is a pleasure in watching something start, continue, and fulfil its potential. That may be fruit growing or one of many other things. But stop and think for a moment: how fruitful is your life? What were you saved for? It is that you may honour God with your life. It is to please the one who loved you and gave himself for you. How fruitful is your life right now?

The preparation of growing fruit

Perhaps you have never thought of it like this, so where do you start? Well, let's keep to the garden metaphor. Imagine you are a gardener and you want to grow fruit. Which fruit do you want to see? What does it need to flourish? Look at the fruits above: Which ones need to be in your life? Which need to be improved? If you are like me, probably all of them. So, make a plan; decide what is or are the priority fruit(s) and decide which ones you want to work on first. What must you do in order that these things will grow, or grow better?

Firstly, the garden needs clearing out. Let's sort out the past. Come to the Lord in earnest prayer and ask him to forgive you again for the lack of fruit in your life. Point out some specific fruits that you long to see more of in your life and ask him for his real help in seeing these fruits grow. Even as you pray, identify what needs to go from the garden. What attitudes, or habits, or sins need to go? What places should be avoided? What about friends or even the job? Is there anything that is stopping or hindering you from seeing these fruits grow? Deal with them, fiercely. Put them away. As the songwriter laments: "*Flowers won't grow in gardens of stone. The ground must be tended, but we left it alone*". Ask the hard questions. Put right what you can, pray about what you can't.

Then, get the seed in: read God's word; hunger for it; pray over it; think about it, ask questions of it. Make sure you're in God's house at every opportunity. Spend time with Christians who you can talk to about the Lord. Do everything you can to get your heart fertile and get the fruit growing.

Does that sound like hard work? It is. No question about it; it is. The hardest part is doing it every day. But the reward is the fruit. The reward is that day by day, starting today (for whoever starts the diet tomorrow doesn't start!) you see growth and change. You will know the Lord's blessing as you walk hand in hand with him. What is the fruit of the Spirit? It is those characteristics that become such an ingrained part of your life that they dominate it. They characterise it. You become that person who lives like this... "he/she is such a joyful person, such a kind person, and so on.

Prayer: Lord help me to start today to sort out my life that I may produce fruit which pleases and honours you. Help me to be honest with you and deal with sins I know I want to keep but I know must go. Amen

84

The fruit of the Spirit is...

The fruit of the Spirit is love...

Galatians 5:22

The garden is dug, the weeds cleared out and the lovely loamy soil is all there and ready, and it looks a lovely sight. It is very satisfying after you have dug the garden or made ready the seed beds and pots, to see nice brown soil all ready to grow. But that is the point; only part of the job is done, nothing is produced yet, and that first part was hard enough! How do you grow spiritual fruit?

Let's lay down a marker here and now: if there is fruit in your life, it is evident. You can see fruit, smell it, touch it, taste it. The word Paul uses here is the same word that John uses when Jesus talks about the vine (John 15). There is no doubt that the fruit is real, ripe and ready. This is important because when we are looking at the fruit of the spirit, they are not things which are ethereal. They are not merely feelings or emotions. They are hard grown; world resistant, devil resistant, really evident things. It is very easy to judge your Christian life by how you feel it's going. Do I feel happy, joyful, at peace and so on? This is <u>not</u> how to measure the fruit of the Spirit.

The first fruit is Love

How does the bible define love? In many ways, but at its root it is sacrificial. *God so loved the world... that he gave*. Love is shown by what you do; 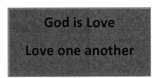 what you do that is not for yourself but for that person who is the object of your love. And, it is done willingly, and with the motive of delighting the person you love. It is done in the context of knowing you are equally loved in return and that the person you love would do and in fact does those same things for you. It is ultimately the perfection of all relationships. It is what makes such a difference in your heart, in your family, in your church and in the world. If you loved perfectly and were loved perfectly like this, it would be the nearest thing to Heaven on earth. But human beings are selfish at heart, and selfishness chokes love.

God loved you even when you didn't love him

God has loved every one of his people before the dawn of the world. This fact is the basis for your relationship with God. It is a guarantee that he will never change his mind and stop loving you. He loves you completely, honestly and without limit. This means you can count on God always loving you as much as it possible for one person to love another. You can trust in God's love. On that rock you can build your relationship. We love him because he first loved us. What does your love for God look like? In practical terms it means you seek to please him and to honour him. What he likes, try to like. What he asks of you, seek to do. In your affections you can never get over why he has loved you and sent his Son to die for you. How is it that there is a mansion in Heaven with your name on? Because God loves you.

God asks you to love his people

This is the even harder bit! It is one thing to love God and to centre your life on him and his glory, but how do you love his people? Well the answer is that he and she are your brother and your sister. They are as loved by God as you are. They are your spiritual kith and kin. If you do not love God's people who you have seen, how can you say you love God whom you have not seen, asks John rhetorically? The fact is the biggest way to express your love for God is to patiently and deliberately set your love on those he has given to accompany you on your march to Zion. They will help you make daily progress if your relationship with them is as God intended it to be. But in return God asks you to help them on their way too. Be a good example. Be interested. Be on the lookout to help. Be prayerful. Be encouraging. Do it to help them and to please the Lord. Sometimes you may ask: "How can I serve God?" It may well be that God is not asking you to lead a meeting, be a preacher, a deacon or any of those "public" things. But you can be absolutely sure he is asking you to love his people, to care for them and encourage them on their way. It is not easy nor is it glamorous but is the biggest proof that you love the Lord. As you get used to doing these things they will become part of who you are. The fruit will always be on the tree.

Prayer: Lord, help me today to examine my heart and see if there is any wicked way in me. Help me to love your people. Help me to know where to start. Help me to swallow my pride and do what it takes to be the one who makes the first move. Help me to keep short accounts with those who hurt me and help me to love as you love me. Amen

88

The fruit of the Spirit is...

The fruit of the Spirit is... joy ...

Galatians 5:22

My brother bought my Dad a number of cheeky posters which he put up in the kitchen. One read: *"If you want to wake up with a smile on your face; go to sleep with a coat-hanger in your mouth!"* The mechanics are ridiculous of course but so is the sentiment. But that expectation for Christians to make out they are always smiling is just as unrealistic. The Christian walk is not about feeling happy, this fruit of joy is about a recognition of what the life really is like. It is a big-picture thing.

The fruit of the Spirit is joy

How does the bible define joy? In the original Greek, Paul uses the word *chara*, which means *calm delight*. So, in this word there is both an emotion (because let's face it emotions are a vital part of our make-up), and soberness; a rational view of things. This explains how we can be joyful when suffering. Look at Paul's letter to the Hebrews:

But recall the former days in which, after you were illuminated, you endured a great struggle with sufferings: partly while you were made a spectacle both by reproaches and tribulations, and partly while you became companions of those who were so treated; for you had compassion on me in my chains, and joyfully accepted the plundering of your goods, knowing that you have a better and an enduring possession for yourselves in heaven.

How could anyone accept the plundering of their goods joyfully? With calm delight? It seems a contradiction. The answer is that these Hebrew Christians saw the big picture. Whilst they clearly suffered in that their goods were taken, they knew that they had – guaranteed – something far better. They looked at and saw what was to come. What happened did not destroy their calm delight because in the eternal perspective, nothing had changed; they still had all they were promised.

Jesus had joy

It's obvious isn't it that the Cross was the most horrible thing imaginable? Physically it was unspeakable agony. Mentally it was tortuous as Jesus heard the cruel taunts of those he came to save. Emotionally, he knew he was on his own, as virtually all forsook him and fled. His mum was there and that must have been agony too. Spiritually for the Lord Jesus a separation from his Father he had never experienced before. So, why did he do it? One reason is for the joy that was set before him. Hebrews 12:2 says:

looking unto Jesus, the author and finisher of our faith, who for the joy that was set before Him endured the cross, despising the shame, and has sat down at the right hand of the throne of God.

Of course it was agony, on every level, but Jesus knew the joy that was coming. So, with calm delight, with deliberate steadfastness, Jesus did the Cross and would not allow the shame of it to take away his joy.

How can you have joy?

What gives a Christian their joy? The Holy Spirit. How does he give it? He gives it as you draw close to him. He gives it as you meditate on what you once were by nature – a child of wrath, and what you are now – a child of grace. That is big-picture

Christianity. All too often it is too easy to focus on the problems of now, real and imagined, and lose that sense of the big picture. If you are going to be a joyful Christian, you have to let go of the idea that you own anything; that you have a right to anything and that you want anything the world has to offer. You must deliberately and irrevocably give them all to Jesus. You must also give him your past, your present and your future. At that point you have the big picture. You know where you come from and where you are going. You know nothing can stop Jesus taking you to Heaven. You know that the Holy Spirit will give you everything you need on the way. That will give you that calm delight. Calmness because you know Jesus has got everything in hand; delight because it is exciting what he has in store for you. Nothing else comes close.

Does it mean we do not care for anyone else, nor for jobs or homes or goods? God grants us fellow-travellers on the way. Each one is to be loved and cared for. Work is a means to live. Do not live to work. Work hard to please the Lord and He will appoint you to the place that is right. Goods and the things of this world are to be viewed in the light of having what we need and what is helpful. But do not spend your time hankering after the things the world tells you is a "must have". The world simply is a bad judge.

Prayer: Lord, help me today to have the right perspective. Help me to see my life in the context of heaven. Fill me today with that calm delight that comes from knowing you. Amen

The fruit of the Spirit is...

The fruit of the Spirit is... peace ...
Galatians 5:22

At the end of the 1960s an anti-war movement was spearheaded by John Lennon and others. Their mantra: *"Give peace a chance"* soon became their war-cry, as they saw the Damocles-esque danger of massive nuclear capability and the insecurity of man's ego-powered itchy trigger-finger. They made the world aware of the danger; but they could not bring peace to a world who seems to delight in war. The Bible has much to say about peace, but a very different peace.

Peace from what?

Jesus the King of glory had his kingdom invaded by Satan the Prince and Pretender to the Throne. His weapons are not swords, guns or bombs but sin, suffering and death. He wanted to be like the Most High. He had so much, yet he wanted more. He rebelled. He was cast out of Heaven like a lightning bolt flashes across the sky. Ever since he has waged a war of implacable hatred against Jesus, his angels and his people.

A leader needs soldiers and God's enemy recruited some of what was the heavenly host, and he has seduced man through Eve and Adam, to join his futile cause. But Jesus came to bruise (break) the head of the enemy and is now reclaiming his soldiers one by one, and Satan can do nothing about it. As the Holy Spirit regenerates each soul their war is ended, and the sinner has joined the Saviour. He has peace with God through the Lord Jesus Christ. The word Paul uses in Romans 5 means literally "to join". The sinner is joined to Jesus and there is everlasting peace. War is over, and peace is permanent. Alongside that peace is a loving relationship which guarantees there will never be war again.

The fruit of the Spirit is peace

But is the Christian life all peace and tranquillity? No, it isn't. Satan is enraged that you have deserted his cause and joined the Lord's. He takes it personally. Bunyan captures the essence of this perfectly in *Pilgrims Progress*: *"How is it that you have run from your king"*, asks Apollyon?

When we "desert" our old captain, army and friends you can be sure that they will do everything they can to try and make you regret it. What they do is target your old sinful nature, the flesh. And the flesh wars against the spirit and the spirit against the flesh. Paul laments that sin is still making him do what he doesn't want to do (Romans 6) and making him feel so, so wretched.

How can you have peace?

You have peace as a gift from the Lord Jesus Christ. He makes peace. He fills you with love for Him and for his people. He gives a calm delight through the storms of life. He joins you to his Church. You and He are one and at one. They are the facts; from those facts comes another aspect of the word for peace [eirēnē] which translates as quietness, or tranquillity. However, this is something like all the fruits which must be worked at or will be lost. You must draw near to God and He will draw near to you. As you walk with and talk with Him those fruits will grow in your heart and life. They will become (your new) second-nature. As in any war you must fight and win to have peace. You need to fight against these things in your heart that would take you away from the Saviour and his will for your life. The more you fight them, the more you have peace in your heart. That is what Paul means when he says: "walk in the spirit and you shall not fulfil the lust of the flesh."

How can you show peace?
Like all the fruits they must have an outward manifestation or they're not fruit! Blessed are those who seek to make peace. That means you must be very slow to take offence and very diligent not to cause offence. It means that you must be determined as far as possible to live in peace with all men. It means when it is the right time [wisdom required!], that you seek to make peace between those who are at war. That is too often the case in families as well as in churches. And your tongue can make a massive difference for good or evil at these junctures. Use your peace with God to bring peace to others. To paraphrase Hendriksen: *you will need this gift to be able to practice the others*.

Prayer: Lord, help me to work hard today to remain at peace with you. Help me to be careful as to what I say and how I say it. Help me to be wise and brave to seek to make peace when you give me opportunity. Amen

96

The Word of the Lord came

The word of the Lord came to Abram, Samuel, Nathan, Gad, Solomon, Jehu, Elijah, Isaiah, Shemiah, Jeremiah, Ezekiel [expressly], Hosea, Joel, Jonah, Micah, Zephaniah, Haggai, Zechariah...

Genesis 15:1 etc.

Have you noticed how God speaks to people in the Bible? Sometimes we read that "The Lord said" [e. g. to Noah Genesis 7:1]. With Moses we have this idiom of "according to the word of Moses". Moses was a unique, and foundational prophet because we read: *the LORD spoke to Moses face to face, as a man speaks to his friend.*

But again and again we have this phrase in the Old Testament, only, that *The word of the Lord came to...* Listed above are some of those men. Some are greatly renowned prophets, such as Elijah and Isaiah, others are some who most bible readers will not remember, such as Shemiah or Gad. How did that happen? What did it look like? How will that help you today?

The Word came

Do you long to hear God speak to you? Wouldn't it wonderful if the Lord spoke to us as he spoke to Adam in the Garden or Moses face to face? Well, those things are to come. Whilst God can do anything, we would not expect him to speak to his people like that today.

But nonetheless, it is important to note that God speaks, and he has always spoken to his people. He initiates the contact. Adam hid but God sought him. Abram was minding his own business in Ur and God called him. Ezekiel was a refugee in hostile Babylon and God came to him. Before you were a Christian, God knew you and He called you to Himself. God speaks. The problem is we don't hear God speak, and perhaps that is in part because we are not expecting it, or we are not listening for it.

We read in Genesis 15 that the word of the Lord came to Abram. How did it come? It was not merely a voice that he heard, a long-distance telephone call, nor a letter. Abram saw Jesus. That is obvious from what comes next: *...the Lord came to Abram in a vision, saying.... But Abram said, 'Lord God what will you give....'"*

Do you see? Abram was holding a conversation with a person. In the Old Testament we see Jesus coming many times in a bodily form: a theophany it is called. And here is one. The word came to Abram. That word was none other than the Lord Himself. That same phrase is used many times to many people. The scriptures were not given in a mystical way; they were given in person on a lot of occasions. How do we know? Listen to John 1:1 & 14:

Jesus is the Word

In the beginning was the Word, and the Word was with God, and the Word was God...And the Word became flesh and dwelt among us.

It may seem amazing, but the truth is that the Old Testament is not separate from the New. There is a unity that is easy to miss. The New is the final part of the story. The Old is the part that sets the scene, gives the problem (sin), and points forward to the solution (the need for righteousness). As Steve Levy writes: *"The righteousness of God is revealed in a new covenant (Jer. 31:31-3); a new Davidic King (Jer. 23:5-6) as well as a new Temple, a new creation[5]"*. The fact is God has always spoken because he always had a plan, and he is constantly executing it. In the past God spoke by his prophets but now in these last days [Jesus is God's final word] has spoken to us by his Son. Jesus is the Word because he is both the messenger and the message. In the end the Bible is all about Jesus; all about his glory, his wonderful person, his amazing redemption and his ultimate triumph; and all of things God invites you to be part of.

Jesus still is the Word

So, to hear Jesus speak, we must use our spiritual eyes, minds and heart. Jesus the Word speaks through the Bible; all of it. Perhaps for many Ezekiel is the hardest book to read, yet the phrase the Word of the Lord  came is found more there than any other book. Do you long to hear Jesus speak to you? Keep reading his word; keep looking for him in his word. See the big picture; the grand plan in his word and it will blow your mind.

May God bless you as you read.

Prayer: Lord, today and always, give me a hunger for your word. Let me see Jesus in all the scriptures. Enlarge my heart and my mind and may what I see change me forever. Amen

---

[5] Bible Overview p.180-1

100

More than a conqueror?

In all these things, we are more than conquerors through Him who loved us.

Romans 8:37

Perhaps today you don't feel so good, spiritually. Perhaps you feel that the enemy is always winning the battle of temptation in your heart and life. Perhaps the life you live feels too hard. The 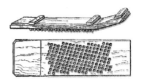 problems are too great. The pressure is always on. Paul likened it to being killed all day long. D M Lloyd Jones[6] writes: *The Romans used to thresh their corn by means of what they called was a tribulum, a kind of sledge or wooden platform with flint or metal teeth underneath.* This picture is used often in the New Testament to describe how Christians are subject to being beaten down; it is what tribulation is. So how can you be being beaten down (threshed, from the French, or thrashed as it's said today), and yet be a conqueror? In fact, you are more than a conqueror. But let's face it; it doesn't always seem that way.

Conquering what?

So, what is it that you are conquering? And what is that going to look like today? To set the context, the first thing that Paul writes about in these last verses of Romans is that the Christian will be hated by the world. Now that looks different across the world

---

[6] Romans 8:17-39 The Final Perseverance of the Saints p.441

and across time. In the reign of Mary 1, (1553-1558) ordinary Christian men and women were burned at the stake. In 1680-88 in Scotland the "Killing Time", as Robert Wodrow called it, saw many Presbyterians lose their lives. Today the "Persecuted Church" in many countries daily face abhorrent treatment for the sake of the gospel. Here and now you may not feel that your problems come too much from the world hating your Christian faith. But just go and try telling those around you their need of a Saviour and see how quickly hostility arises! How do you conquer that?

Then, there is the enemy of your soul. He constantly wages war against you. He is the accuser of the brethren. He is always in your ear telling you why you cannot, will not go to Heaven. How do you conquer someone so much more powerful than you: someone who knows and watches for your weaknesses, so he can try to trip you up again and again?

Then there is the sin in your heart: how wretched it is. Paul is not the only one to cry out in anguish over his inclination to sin; it is a cry every Christian echoes. How do you conquer that?

Conquering how?

You conquer through the love of Christ. *We are more than conquerors through him that loved us*, Paul writes in triumph. What does that mean? It is through the Lord Jesus that you conquer the world's hatred, Satan's enmity and your own sinful weakness. Jesus' love is a castle against the world; a fire-suit against the enemy's burning hatred and it is both a cleansing balm and a motivational armour against sin. The simple truth is: you love him because he first loved you. His love for you is eternal, unquenchable and full of fervour. You need to grab hold of that love; to open the door to it, because the more you experience that love, the more you will love him. That is when you know your greatest victories. Jesus love for you is an unanswerable, unshakeable, unconquerable weapon. It's yours for the using. Draw near to God and he will draw near to you. Conquering how? It's not easy, but it is simple and profound. Keep conquering sincerely, earnestly today and see what change it makes. It will be remarkable.

Today, come to God in prayer. Ask him to show you his love in action in your heart. Ask him to help you love him more and more. Begin the practice of seeking **_Him_** personally, experientially not formally and habitually as we all often do. Have a vital relationship with the Lord – that same Lord Jesus who amazingly stands at the door and knocks! How can that be? It is so because he didn't die for an abstract cause; he died for you because he loves you more than you can ever realise. His love makes you more than a conqueror. You won't limp or stagger into heaven. You will march like a victor. You will triumph like a general. Whatever attacks you from without or within Jesus love will enable you to triumph over all of it.

Prayer: Lord, today help me draw near, really near to you. May my love grow deeper today and every day as I see you working in my life, changing me bit by bit into the person you died for me to be. Amen.

104

The Temple of God

And there I will meet with the children of Israel, and the tabernacle shall be sanctified by My glory. So I will consecrate the tabernacle of meeting and the altar... I will dwell among the children of Israel and will be their God.

Exodus 29:43-45

What do you think of when you think of the Temple of God? Do images of a sand-ridden tent that Moses put up in the desert, the grand Temple of Solomon or the little one of Haggai come to mind? This study might surprise you if that is the case, because the temple is something more than that.

The first temple

What is a temple? It is the place where God dwells with man. It is a place of communion. A place where worshipful fellowship can take place.

With that definition in mind, it follows that the first temple was the Garden of Eden. Adam Mabry writes: *The Garden of Eden... was more than God's interesting botanical garden. It was the first true temple – a place where humans dwelt with God perfectly*[7]. God at the very beginning of the world, shows mankind he wants to dwell with them. That is (in part) why he made the world in the first place. God entered that temple housing Adam and Eve.

---

[7] The Art of Rest p. 27

A different temple was needed

But sin drove man out and that temple was destroyed. But a desire to worship God is implanted in our hearts – even though it is imperfect, as the many altars on Mars Hill in the apostle Paul's day testifies. As men went about their lives, they built altars; they sought and craved fellowship with God. That is why it was such an incredible promise that God made to the children of Israel in Exodus 29:45: *I will dwell among the Children of Israel and will be their God.* What a privilege. So, how could this happen now that sin had entered the world? Since God cannot look upon nor dwell with sin  and those who commit sin, and since we are powerless to deal with it, God has opened a way. It is through a sacrifice. So, in time a Tabernacle was made, and a Temple was built, but they could not be permanent, since they were made with human hands. As a reminder of this the Lord put a woven cherub on the curtain leading to the Holy of Holies, to remind them of why the curtain was needed at all (Exodus 26:31). It was a cherub that prevented Adam getting back to the Garden.

This temple was the temple of meeting; the place where God's people could meet with him. Israel first and then the Gentiles also.

Where is the temple now?

The temple is gone, and it has not and will not be rebuilt. This is because Jesus has come and completed all the temple pointed toward and put in place the foundation for the ultimate temple. That is why the curtain was torn in two from top to bottom. You see; you are the temple of God. Amazing isn't it? Look at Paul's words: *Do you not know that you are the temple of God and that the Spirit of God dwells in you?* Jesus has died so that is sin dealt with once and for all. The Holy Spirit has come and made you alive, and he lives in you. In fact, Jesus said that through him, both he and the Father live in you. You have the capacity to have true and incredible fellowship with God. And there is more: The bible says that this is a deposit guaranteeing the Fullness of what is to come.

Another temple?

Yes. One day you will go to be with the Lord, or He will come and take you and all his people to be with himself. There will be a new heaven, and a new earth, but no temple, *for the dwelling of God is with men (Revelation 21:3-4).* So, Eden is restored. We have gone full circle, but with one massive and vital difference. There will never be another victory for the devil. No more sin, nor crying, nor tears nor death. The Garden won't be the temple, but God himself will be. We will dwell with him, and nothing will ever corrupt it, for nothing can defeat the Omnipotent God. You are God's temple. You are what Eden was meant to be and a foretaste of what God has in store. Today you must look after this temple carefully. You belong to God: make sure you don't defile his temple by bringing in sin, and anything which spoils your fellowship with God.

Prayer: Lord, today help me to realise what an amazing thing you have done for. Help to me rejoice with gratitude that you have chosen to live with me. Help me to delight and honour that privilege in how I live. Amen

108

Convocations and Intermissions

S
ix days shall work be done, but the seventh day is a Sabbath of
solemn rest, a holy convocation. You shall do no work on it; it is
the Sabbath of the LORD in all your dwellings.

Leviticus 23

Today... have a rest

Can I suggest that you read this page either on a Sunday morning or, **for** a Sunday morning! Today we are talking about the necessity of rest. The Lord built that into our DNA, and we need it. Today, as in many previous generations, the enemy of souls doesn't want us to rest. He would rather we burn out and be useless. But, reader, hear me (or rather, read me) out.

The children of Israel were chosen by God to enter into a covenant with him. This was a unique privilege for the nation, and it carried an awesome responsibility. There were lots of laws, rituals and ceremonies but two things stand out first. These two things were:

a) meeting with the Lord: a convocation
b) that of rest: a sabbath

You might say: "so what" but as a Christian, you are not exempt from keeping the Ten Commandments: they are universal and will form the basis of the Judgement. But also, as a Christian, you are to know the principles that lay behind the law and all the ceremonial aspects and see what they teach. You do not – and cannot – earn your salvation from them, but they are there like a schoolmaster to lead you into a deeper relationship with Christ. Let's look at some words...

What is a Covenant?

The word **covenant** comes from a root word meaning a *cutting*; which means literally, "a *compact,* made by passing between *pieces* of flesh". In other words, two people joined together by blood. God initiated a covenant and ratified it by a lamb. He did this with Abraham (Genesis 15) and he continued to do it right through until the time of Moses when at Passover time, the people of Israel became His. He redeemed them from bondage to Egypt. He rescued them from the wrath (of Pharaoh) then and to come. We are part of a new "cutting"; a new covenant, sealed by the blood of Jesus.

What is a Convocation?

This special relationship that Israel had with God, meant that they were to meet together. These meetings were called holy convocations and they either preceded or were part of the appointed feasts. In other words, they were special appointments with the Lord: for *feast* literally means an appointment; and a *convocation* carries with it the idea of a rehearsal. We would interpret that alongside the New Testament teaching that all these things pointed forward to a time when the redeemed people by Christ could literally meet with the Lord, their covenant God.

What is a Sabbath?

There is an instruction built into the very fabric of Old Testament life that there had to be an honouring of the seventh day. It was a sabbath – *shabawth.* That word literally means *an intermission.* So as a principle, the people of God were to have an intermission from the ordinary things of life, and in place of the ordinary things of life they were to have a whole day as an appointment with God. At the Feast times they were to have a sabbath-style rest time literally *shabawthone:* a special holiday. All of that was based on the rest principle enshrined in the fourth commandment.

What is the sabbath for?

There are four principles of sabbath day rest to pick up on:

It was a **sacred** day: set apart *for* the Lord.

It was a **rest** day: a day to be spent *with* the Lord.

It was a **sacrificial** day: a day to give *to* the Lord.

It was a **selfless** day: a day to *please* the Lord.

Have a careful, thoughtful look at these four principles, which are still in force for all Christians, and work out some real practical suggestions on how you might use the Rest Day wisely. If you look at them properly, it will change your Sunday. If it changes your Sunday; it will change your life.

Prayer: Lord, today help me to see how important your day – the Lord's Day – is. Help me to cherish it as a gift. Help me to use it for my good, other people's good and for your glory. Amen

Sort it out

I implore Euodia and I implore Syntyche to be of the same mind in the Lord

Philippians 4:2

A bit of a bust up

It's true isn't it that you are not surprised when a non-believer gives you a hard time for your faith. If you have been laughed at, passed over in favour of someone else; been the victim of a practical "joke" it isn't nice, but, it happens. You can pray about it, talk to Christian friends about it, and as you reflect upon it you know that is what you expect as a Christian to happen. It's always been that way and it will be until Jesus comes again. The comfort is that as long as you have obeyed Paul's words in Romans 12:18: *If it is possible, as much as depends on you, live peaceably with all men,* you know that the Lord knows, cares, protects and even uses it for his glory.

But, what about when you have had a bust up with another Christian? There is no such comfort is there? In theory you say: Well that shouldn't happen should it? But it does. And when it does it can be the hardest of things to understand, cope with and to solve. Looking at Philippians 4 it seems that these two hard-working women had had a bust up. Paul implores them to sort it out. He even urges the pastor and another worker, Clement, to help in the matter. What happened we are not told but coupling that incident with Paul and Barnabas in Acts 15 and Paul and Peter in Galatians 2 you can see that Christians fall out.

It happens because of strongly held beliefs

Sometimes this happens because people hold different view about the same thing. You start to paddle in different directions. This is a great trick of the enemy. Usually the things that you argue over are not the big, core teaching of the Bible, but over something quite small. However, at the time it seems a big thing. You sincerely hold your view; they sincerely hold theirs. You cannot agree and it all goes wrong. You start to find allies to your view (usually under the heading of: what do you think about ..., or doesn't the bible say...., or even guess what *they* said to me...) and they do likewise. It can cause hurt and even a division in the church, much to the consternation of the Holy Spirit.

It happens because of sin, pride and selfishness

But, worse than this, sometimes it happens over time, and it is about the differences between you and another. Differences of personality, background, position in the church and strength of character. A new member joins and you feel that everyone listens to them rather than you who has been at the church a long time. Or maybe you are that "new kid on the block". Those conflicts usually are the result of pride. Perhaps it is simply that you want your own way – or they do. That is selfishness. Perhaps you cannot forgive them for something in the past – or they cannot forgive you. That is sin, as we are expressly told by the Lord Jesus to forgive one another. This is not an exhaustive list: there may be 101 reasons for you and another to fall out.

The key thing is to examine your motives and make sure they are right before the Lord. Be slow to take offence, for many things are said either in jest or without any intention to hurt.

How do you sort it out?

First of all, ask: do you want to – or are you still clinging either to you being right or you being victim? Then, be quick to apologise for what you have said and done that could have been hurtful. Examine your motives and lay them out before the Lord. If you have been hurt, be quick to forgive. Do everything you can to make it right; to be of one mind. If it is really important speak to the pastor, or if he is the problem speak to an elder or a mature Christian (who must be independent!).

The second step is to take that person with you to seek a resolution. The third is to consider whether to tell it to the church.

But understand that it's an imperfect church, made up of imperfect people and it may be that you never are forgiven, or that you never agree. What then? Always do what you can to keep the relationship open and loving. Keep praying for that person, for it is hard to quarrel with someone for whom you pray for. Actively leave it with the Lord and let the Lord of the church deal with what you cannot. In all you make sure it is done to honour the Lord and in time you'll see him honour you.

Prayer: Lord, help me to remember your command to forgive as I have been forgiven, and to put it behind me and move on as much as it lies in me. Help me to bear it if someone will not forgive me. Amen

Does God exist?

In the beginning God... In the beginning was the Word....
Genesis 1:1 and John 1:1

The Existence of God

Have you ever been asked: "Does God exist"? Or perhaps the same question another way: "How do you know that God exists?" Sometimes it is asked with an agenda to discredit you. But sometimes it may be asked with a genuine desire to hear an answer. So, how do you answer, apart from just saying "yes" of course!

When we look at how the Bible starts we read: *"In the beginning God..."*
There are two things to notice: firstly, the Bible does not here, or anywhere else,  seek to prove the existence of God: it simply makes the statement that he does. It is what we might call an assumptive statement, or a presupposition. These are the facts. They are not in dispute: they are the foundation block for all the Universe. The second presupposition is that God reveals Himself in his word. So, the Bible has as its basis God exists and that he reveals himself to the world through his Word. When you witness, use those presuppositions. Do not seek to prove the existence of God.

I emphasize this because you will read, and hear, those who try to prove the existence of God rationally. But God never tries to prove his existence. We have a God who has revealed himself, and we accept the existence of God by faith. And that faith must be rightly and reverently fed from the Scriptures.

What is God like?

But what is God like? This is a study of course that would (and will) last forever. It is inexhaustible. Isaiah asks rhetorically: *To whom then will you liken God? Or what likeness will you compare to Him?*

The best option is to look at Jesus who said, *"he who has seen me has seen the Father"*. That is why John starts his Gospel "in the beginning was the Word. It's a deliberate, albeit implicit, way of telling us that Jesus is God. What does John say about Jesus? Jesus is the Word. Why do you and I use words? You use them in two ways: firstly, you think in words; it is the way you articulate what is in your mind. Then you formulate and translate what you want to communicate using words.

Secondly, you use words to convey your message: what it is you want to say. So, when John says that Jesus is the Word of God: he is saying that Jesus is the avenue that God articulates all that He is and all that he wants to say to men and women. Read Proverbs 8:27-31 for an expansion of this. Hebrews 1 is a good commentary:

God who at various times and in various ways spoke in time past to the fathers by the prophets, has in these last days spoken to us by his Son, whom he has appointed heir of all things, through whom also he made the worlds who being in

the brightness of his glory and the express image of his person, who upholding all things by the word of his power... when he had by himself purged our sins, sat down at the right hand of the majesty on high (Hebrews 1:1-3).

So, if you want to know God; study Jesus. If you want to make God known use the teaching and the life of Jesus.

A relationship with God

But John's message has a point to make: that is Jesus came to reveal God so that we might have life in his name. Jesus came for a purpose and that is to save sinners. Theology must always be relevant. He wrote to convince his readers that Jesus is the Son of God and to believe it that they would have eternal life in his name. Do you believe this with your whole heart? Do you believe that this is the most important thing that you embrace? If it is, how is it affecting your life, priorities and behavior? Nothing and no-one can ever come between you and your Saviour. God exists. He exists and occupies the Universe – in fact the Universe (Psalm 19) is but a mere piece of handiwork to him. God exists: He lives in the heart of each of his children, now and always.

Prayer: Lord, help me to be sure you are my God. Help me today to be unashamed believer. Help me to make you known. Amen

120

Go and make disciples

If I be lifted up I will draw all men to me.

John 13:32

Have you ever puzzled at the words of Jesus in Matthew 28:20, where He says: *Go into all the world and make disciples?* First of all, not all are called to be missionaries. Also, there is the much deeper problem which is; you cannot save a single soul. So how do you carry out this command?

An unlikely partnership
Many Christians on a Sunday will hear or say the words of "the grace…" in II Corinthians 13:14. When we come to the part; *"and the fellowship (or communion) of the Holy Spirit"*, do you know what you are asking for? That word means partnership and it teaches that you as a child of God are in partnership with him in the work of the gospel. That is breath-taking really isn't it? The God who said "let the light shine" is allowing you; asking you to join in the work of his kingdom. Why is that so? God patently doesn't need anyone to do anything if He can create the world from nothing. So, then what is your part? It is, to use the words of our text, to lift up Jesus.

An unlikely illustration
In Numbers 21:4-9 the children of Israel had sinned by complaining against God. They continually charged God with the very opposite of what he was doing. They said that God had brought them out

of Egypt to die in this wretched desert. God in fact had brought them out to save them, cherish them and choose them as his own people. Such ingratitude! The criticism is almost blasphemous: it is a low point in their history. The snakes that were in that part of the desert came in force and bit the people. They were dying and cried out in repentance. In grace and mercy God said to put up a snake on a pole. All who were bitten just had to look at the snake on the pole and they would live. And that is what they did.

Now that could be just left as a rather gruesome story from the Old Testament were it not for the fact that Jesus takes this story and explains how it is relevant and vital. He told Nicodemus: *And as Moses lifted up the serpent in the wilderness, even so must the Son of Man be lifted up, that whoever believes in Him should not perish but have eternal life.*

An unlikely position

Now that is not the last time that Jesus alluded to this story. In John 12:32 he told his disciples as our text says, that he needed to be lifted up. In other words, he had to die. The disciples simply do not understand. But there are two essential things to point out.

Jesus had to die that you might be saved. He had to be lifted up, not on a pole, but on a Roman Cross. He needed to be put between God and man, so to speak, to re-build the bridge between them that was destroyed by sin. But also, he needed to be paraded. When he was lifted up, everyone could see him. Probably 8 feet up off the ground on a hill; most people would have seen Jesus. He needed to be lifted up to be seen.

An essential partnership

Now, physically Jesus needed to be lifted up. But spiritually, or rather evangelistically speaking, Jesus needs to be lifted up. If he is he will draw all (types of) men to himself in faith and repentance. So, when Jesus tells you and his church to go and make disciples, and when Paul says this work is a partnership: what is your part? It is to lift Jesus up. That means to talk about him, but also to live unashamedly in the way he asks. That honours him too.

So today ask: how can I make Jesus known? How can I lift him up? What will honour him? What might dishonour him? You may not be the next Edwards, Spurgeon or Judson, but you are put where you are by the Lord for a reason and however unlikely it seems, in your life and situation today there are opportunities. We can do nothing on our own; it's a partnership, but we can do all things through Him who strengthens us.

Today, then in your "corner of the vineyard" seek to lift Jesus up. Seek to please him, honour him, especially in the so-called little things, and talk about how much he does, has done and will do for you. No-one can take away your testimony. Seek to lift Jesus up and be sure that he will do his part and draw people to Himself. Does it sound unlikely? It does, but it's what Jesus said would be his way of working. So, go with faith in the Father, the peace of the Son, and the partnership and of the Spirit. God bless.

Prayer: Lord, help me want to lift Jesus up. Help to know how. Please give me the courage, wisdom and strength. For your glory. Amen

Daily Progress

Why write a book of daily readings? Well, do you know the story of Goldilocks? When she ate the porridge, it was firstly too hot, then too cold, but the third was just right, and so it went on with the chair and the bed. This book was written with a desire to provide something that was neither too much or too little, but "just right". When you read something each day, you do not need it to be so complicated you fall asleep, or too bland you forget it as soon as you finish. The aim with this book is provide something that is useful, challenging and relevant, all in two sides of paper!

The Bible describes what Christians **"are"**; what they should **"be"** and what they should **"do"**. Why is this so? It is so because you and I are saved to glorify the Lord who loved us and gave himself for us. It is so because we are saved to make a difference to this lost and sin-stained world. It is so because we are called to make daily progress in the Christian life.

Being a Christian is not a passive thing but an active thing. However, we need to neither be "too hot" to handle nor "too cold" to be useful, but "just right". You must be a relevant witness, a faithful servant and a mature believer, rightly handling the word of life and truth as you explain it to others. This book will help you as you read it on a daily basis, or as a book you can return to again and again for comfort, guidance and to be challenged.

Gary Stevens has been preaching and teaching for 40 years and trained at the Grace Baptist Seminary in Suffolk. He is married to Jill and is also the author of:

The Pilgrims Psalmgress

Ordinary Christians, Extraordinary Progress

Daily Progress II

These can be bought at Amazon or the website below. A booklet:

What is God all about? aiming to explain the gospel simply and with jargon can only be bought at the website *www.garybstevens.co.uk*

Printed in Great Britain
by Amazon

37807114R00076